Also by
Stephanie Rosenbaum

Kids in the Kitchen: Fun Food

Honey: From Flower To Table

Anti-Bride Guide:
Tying the Knot Outside of the Box

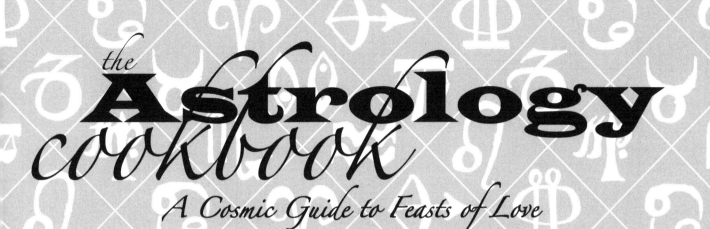

the Astrology cookbook

A Cosmic Guide to Feasts of Love

Stephanie Rosenbaum

Manic D Press · San Francisco

For information, address Manic D Press, Inc., PO Box 410804, San Francisco CA 94141.
www.manicdpress.com   ISBN 978-1-933149-26-4

Book design and illustration by Justine Ives
Female cover and food illustrations by Dodeskaden

Printed in the USA

Table of Contents

The **Star-Kissed** *Kitchen*

L onging for a Leo? Crushed out on a Capricorn? Whether you're angling for the cute guy in class or the gorgeous redhead at the puppy park, there are dozens of ways to make that first move. Chat, smile, find some alluring common interest, and then ask him out to that Swedish vampire movie. Take her to a Lykke Li concert, go out to breakfast at 3 a.m., leave a splash of glitter down the steps. Whatever it takes.

Where this book comes into play is a few days, or weeks, later, when you're ready for that all-important dinner date. Actually, it doesn't have to be dinner. It could be brunch, a barbecue, even a picnic in the park. What's important is you and your would-be sweetie, close together, dewy-eyed and ready to be fed. And best of all, you're cooking.

Yes, you. You may think this is better left to the professionals, the trained chefs and menu-writers and their attendant water-pourers and napkin-folders. Restaurants do have their getting-to-know-you place, but once you're past the third or four date, it's time to get your honey home. Your home, and to be exact, your kitchen.

As a restaurant critic who took a lot of people out to eat under the cover of doing my job, I can tell you straight that when it comes to getting someone to fall in love with you, dinner at the fanciest joint in town is nothing compared to homemade red beans and rice at your own kitchen table. (And if you can follow it up with homemade pie—well, you better have an extra toothbrush in the medicine cabinet right now.) Dinner… pie… waffles in the morning: these work, I promise you.

Then again, why not make really, really sure? How can you cook your sweetheart exactly the meal that will make their heart sing? Asking is no good. Why? Because few people will admit what they really like. "Oh, you know, anything, maybe pasta?" is as much of a demand as most guests will make. So don't listen to them. But still, you need guidelines. And that's where astrology comes in. A single casual inquiry ("Hey, when's your birthday?") and bingo! You'll have their needs, their wants, their likes and dislikes nailed.

Of course, serious students of astrology would insist that a sun sign (where the sun was in the zodiac on the day of one's birth) is only the most obvious and unsubtle aspect of a horoscope, and to truly know someone, you have to know what houses their planets are in, where their moon is and what their rising sign is. All true. But for the purpose of dinner and romance, knowing just a sun sign will do.

In the chapters that follow, you'll find descriptions of each sign. You'll discover their personality traits at the table and in the bedroom, how they like to be enticed, and how to plan a menu of perfect seduction. You'll learn the elements, and the planets that rule them, and what characteristics they share.

Now, to explain: each sun sign has its general characteristics and qualities, influenced by three aspects. First is the ruling planet: Mercury, Venus, Mars, Jupiter, Saturn, Uranus, Neptune, and Pluto, plus the Sun and Moon. The vibe of each planet, like a gravitational orbit, influences the sign from afar. These are the deep guiding forces that shape a life in the long run.

Spread out over the 12 signs, the four basic elements of fire, air, water, and earth form the bedrock of each sign's character.

Aries, Leo, and Sagittarius—the signs of Fire—thrive on conflagration and drama, and are always looking for ways to raise the temperature, whether that means heating it up at home or burning it up on the dance floor.

Libra, Gemini, and Aquarius are often the creative powerhouses of the zodiac. Ideas from brilliant to goofy swirl through the ether, and with their heads happily up in the clouds, these Air signs are perfectly positioned to catch all of them.

Born with their feet on the ground—that's Taurus, Virgo, and Capricorn. These Earth signs are often intensely practical, domestic, and grounded. Need a shoulder to lean on? These are the ones to take care of you.

Awash in Water, Pisces, Scorpio, and Cancer follow the emotional currents, riding the waves up and down through temperamental storms and dark forces that others can only guess at, reflecting back both good and bad. But when all is well, the Water signs are as blissful as a perfect day at the beach.

Finally, each sign also comes with a quality, depending on where it falls within the season. Think of these as birth-order influences, shaping both character and day-to-day behavior. They are divided by Cardinal (first), Fixed (middle), and Mutable (last). In spring, for example, cardinal sign Aries comes first, ready to jump in and be at the head of pack. Taurus, a fixed sign, comes next, firmly wedged in the middle, the center around which everything revolves (or so they wish). Last comes mutable Gemini, always looking ahead, longing to grab the next new thing.

Each season starts with a Cardinal sign: Aries (spring), Cancer (summer), Libra (autumn), and Capricorn (winter). These are the signs of leadership and taking charge. They don't necessarily have to own the show, but they sure do want to run it, and those around them often turn to them as natural leaders (and tops).

At the middle of each season is a Fixed sign: Taurus (spring), Leo (summer), Scorpio (autumn), and Aquarius (winter). These are the signs of the boss, the man or woman in charge, who knows how it's all supposed to be. Rock solid even under pressure, they also know to manage the people around them to achieve their ends, all for their own good, of course. Family and tradition, however defined, are deeply important to them. This doesn't make them conservative, necessarily, just staunch defenders of their hearth and home, or at least, really great decorators.

Straddling the end of one season and the beginning of another are the Mutable signs: Gemini (spring/summer), Virgo (summer/autumn), Sagittarius (autumn/winter), and Pisces (winter/spring). Duality, adaptiveness, and flexibility are the hallmarks of these signs of change. Sudden decisions—like a storm that sweeps through to strip the autumn branches bare, or weather that flares from parka-chilly to popsicles-in-the-park overnight—may not happen every day, but when they do, watch out: these Mutable signs can cut and run to you (or away from you) in a flash.

Now, back to the kitchen. If you do your job right (menu perfectly chosen, food alluring, banter smart and amusing), you're sure to be invited over to return the favor. And that's why you need this list, not just the recipes following. The way you, Virgo woman, like to cook and serve won't be the same as how your Capricorn man does it. Butch Scorpio, different from femme Aquarius. Two Taurus dudes, hey, go for it (just don't make any plans outside the house for the next three days).

What's for Dinner?

Aries combines a hard-charging, make-an-impact drive to change the world with an intense domesticity. They're often fantastic cooks, when they want to be. They'll buckle down to a family routine of spaghetti on Tuesdays and goulash on Fridays if they must, but they're most satisfied when they can make a splash. Cherry pie to make your lover weep and moan at your grave when you're gone; chicken braised with three heads of garlic; salmon doused with port, rosemary, and brown sugar; chocolate martinis... you get the picture. The caveat? Don't tell Aries what to do in his or her own kitchen. (Actually, this is always good advice, no matter what the sign.) So what if you're a Top Chef and your sweetie is reading the directions on the Rice-A-Roni? Sit down, shut up, and bask. They're the studs. Let them show off, no matter how the tomatoes get chopped in the process.

Taurus is here to sweep you off your feet, darling. Sugar daddy (or sugar mama) will take care of you, ply you with lavish treats, and wrap you in satin leopard pajamas. How this happens? Well, Taurus is about the big picture, not the little details. It may take a while for that steak to get the table, but you're sure to be amused in the interim. Bring some glamorous snacks, though, since speedy delivery is not the Taurus way, unless they're ordering in (always a possibility, if only so they can eat their cake and have you, too). Caviar, smoked salmon, fancy French pâté, smoked oysters: if it's rich, salty, and silky on the tongue, it's made for Taurus.

If *Gemini* needs one how-to guide in the kitchen, it's Pam Anderson's *How to Cook Without a Book*. (No, not that Pam Anderson. Perhaps in the future, "cookbook writer" and "tattooed ex-wife of Tommy Lee" won't be mutually exclusive, but not yet.) Of course, Gemini would probably never read something so boringly prescriptive. What stimulates their countertop creativity is a wide-open window into another culture (or three). Always questing, Gemini isn't satisfied with mere culinary tourism. Adventurous of palate, they'll go for the gusto, slicing up blood sausage or shaving fresh turmeric with aplomb. Don't ask for a menu beforehand, since finding inspiration in the moment is the Gemini way in both the kitchen and the bedroom. It may take some time, but their creative fireworks will make it all worthwhile.

Cancer will wait until they're sure of their (and your) intentions before opening up that hard shell. But once you've been invited in, the world's your oyster. You'll be treated to all the delicacies they can find, served without pretense or fuss. Want to pick up that asparagus with your fingers? Let plum juice run down your chin? That's sexy (and cute) to Cancer. Roll up your sleeves and dig in with these homebodies, who always prefer a meal in to a dinner out. Because, of course, when you're dining at home, the bedroom (or the couch or the sheepskin rug) is just steps away from the table. And hot summer lovin' is always the best dessert for these June/July babies.

Leo is firing up the barbecue just for you so, baby, come hungry. Just follow the scent of smoke & grease, since Leo basks in the heat of a good conflagration. If they can't grill, they'll flambée. These heat-seeking lions love to feed a crowd, but they'll happily put their charms to work on you for a special tête-à-tête. Like their namesakes, most Leos love that meaty goodness, so come prepared to gnaw some bones. Expect big flavors with big impact, like garlic, butter, meat, and chocolate. You don't need to bring a host or hostess gift when you come to dinner at Leo's house. Just your fine self (in flaming red panties or silky boxers) and your enthusiasm for your king or queen of the savannah should be enough.

Virgos are dedicated domestic geniuses. Whether they're naturals in the kitchen or not, you can always count on getting a lovely meal at Virgo's well-set table. These are people who go to the experts to learn what they want to know, so expect to see lots of cookbooks and good-quality implements lining the shelves of their tidy and welcoming kitchens. And if there's no time to cook? No worries. They know where to shop, and their impulses are generous. The one zero-tolerance rule? No flakiness! Making a date with Virgo means you show up on time in a clean shirt, with a pretty box of chocolates in your hands. Frantic texting about the traffic on the freeway or your parking woes won't earn any points here. If Virgo—like Buffy the Vampire Slayer—can make time for romance in between saving the world, you can ring the doorbell when you promised.

Libra likes to make everything look easy, and they want their lip gloss to look perfect while they do it. But cooking is a messy business, and they can be a little embarrassed by the state of their kitchen during the initial git-'r-done phase, what with the raw chicken dripping on the cutting board, the papery bits of garlic skin flying around, and flour all over the floor. So, if Libra's cooking you dinner, don't arrive early. Wait until the cooking's all over but the sexy time. When there's nothing left to do but slicking the salad with olive oil or drizzling Amaretto over the berries, walk in with flowers and a kiss. Sit down, have a glass of something, and keep Libra entertained while dinner wafts to the table. Don't jump in to help, don't try to do the dishes (revealing their messes is not the Libra way), and if you need something, ask for it rather than rummaging around in the fridge. Remember, Libras are the hosts of the zodiac, and helping yourself will make them feel like their hospitality has been tried and found wanting. Oh, and always ask if they'd like you to bring cupcakes. Libras *love* cupcakes!

Scorpios can smell fear. Despite their down-and-dirty reputation, they won't hurt you. Oh, no… but they will lure you into the danger zone, where you'll suddenly find yourself downing barbecued eel or blood sausage or hot-pepper-fried crickets. Whatever your gastronomic fear factor is, Scorpio will find it out, and make you not only confront it but love it. Fun, huh? You bet, and that's only the beginning. Can't stand the heat? Then you don't want to be in the kitchen (or up on the table) with the Scorp. One-up your Scorpio lover, if you dare. They'll try anything once, and their pride trumps any secret squeamishness every time. Kangaroo kebabs? Pig's ears? Corn fungus (*huitalacoche*, to those familiar with this Mexican delicacy)? Bring it along, but only if you truly adore it, since the heights and depths of passion light Scorpio's fire.

Sagittarius—maestro or train wreck? As the optimist of the zodiac, Sag's attitude in the kitchen is, "Hey, what could happen?" And as anyone who's ever tried their hand at pie crust knows… many, many interesting outcomes await when you step into the kitchen, not all of them edible. Restless, self-confident Sag is the one who'll decide on the spur of the moment to deep-fry a turkey, smoke a whole salmon, or make wasabi sorbet. Their energy can be infectious, and somehow they manage to sail through on sheer chutzpah. When they work (which is most of the time), Sag meals are spectacular. When they don't, the failures are often equally awe-inspiring, and worth it just for the story. Go ready to celebrate their triumph—or order pizza if that three-day French Laundry recipe goes belly-up.

Capricorn probably doesn't spend a lot of time in the kitchen, even as they claim to crave a home life. Given their workaholic, perfectionist tendencies (along with the fact that they save entrance to their lair for a select group), expect top-quality appliances and nothing but champagne and last week's Kung Pao chicken in the fridge. But once they get used to inviting you over, they'll take that cardinal, earth-rooted energy and charge ahead. With a taste for the best, they'll take pleasure in finding the sweetest peaches and juiciest tomatoes for you. Who needs a cookbook? Solid, satisfying eats, that's what you'll get at Chez Cap. Bring along a good bottle of wine (or a carton of ice cream for their secret sweet tooth), and feel free to help them track down where they last stashed the salad spinner.

Aquarius is a cascade of ideas, and the kitchen is one of the best places for these water-bearers to pour out their brilliance. As the trekkers of the zodiac, they've sampled a multitude of cuisines at the source, and they love nothing more than sharing what they learned walking through the plazas of Lima or the piazzas of Bologna. Their cabinets are a United Nations of exotic condiments, liquors, and seasonings from Croatia and Turkey to Thailand and Bali. Cookbooks may be piled up on their shelves, but their best creations come from their own ever-inventive minds. Peanut butter pizza? Sea urchin for breakfast? Come with an open mind, ready to be delighted. Want to impress? Bring something they've never tasted before, dip in a finger, and offer to slip it between their lips.

Pisces may seem dreamy, but they're often surprisingly precise in the kitchen. Just like salmon following the same route back to their spawning grounds year after year, Pisces likes to follow recipes, and if they're missing those 2 tablespoons of minced cilantro, they'll put on their shoes and go find them rather than throw in parsley instead. Try to jostle Pisces out of their routines if that's your bag; otherwise, enjoy what you get: a carefully presented, well thought-out meal, served with the full accoutrements of romance. Pisces doesn't mind putting in some time to get reality and their notions of romance to coalesce, which can mean flickering candles, fresh flowers, matching placemats, even folded hand towels in the powder room. Bring along a few cherished rose-colored fantasies of your own, and they'll be happy to oblige.

Getting *Started*

Most of the dishes in this book can be whipped up pretty easily, without a lot of fancy-pants ingredients or equipment. Roll a pie crust out with a wine bottle, make beef stew with Two-Buck Chuck, scavenge a corner bodega for hors d'oeuvres: speaking from experience, you can do any of these things, and still get lucky in (and out) of the kitchen.

If your general happiness requires close proximity to takeout Thai food, French movies, late-night bookstores, and weird little shops selling nothing but vintage buttons or stuffed dead mice in tiny tutus, your adult life will probably be spent in a city. And this means that for at least your first few years, you'll probably be living in a tiny studio apartment with a kitchen the size of a tissue box, or sharing a large, grubby house with five roommates, all nuking popcorn or making stir-fries at the same time in an equally grubby and crowded kitchen. Frills like dishwashers, adequate counter space, and room for espresso machines and food processors may be well beyond your resources.

Weep not! With good cheer, ingenuity and inventiveness, you can always get dinner on the table, to say nothing of peach pie and coconut crème caramel. It's true a soufflé looks more Parisian puffing up over the edge of a fluted white porcelain soufflé dish, but it will puff up just as nicely in whatever Pyrex or china bowls you might already have around the house.

Great ingredients will reward you, and good equipment can make cooking easier. But by the same token, expensive gear and fancy condiments won't make you a better cook, so you might as well learn how you like to cook with just the basics. Anything a food processor can do, a knife, a cutting board, a box grater, and your two hands can do just as easily, with less clean-up. Unless you need to make potato pancakes for 100, you can do any and all chopping, dicing, or shredding jobs faster and easier without having to assemble, fill, and clean one of those space-hogging behemoths.

Spend your money on the stuff that matters—beautiful raspberries and melons in season, when their scent alone can ring the pleasure centers of your brain like a lit-up pinball machine; fresh meat and eggs from humanely-raised, pasture-fed animals; real cheese and bread; dewy vegetables bought locally from the people who grew them. In doing so, you'll not only be feeding yourself and your friends and neighbors, you'll be digging into your community, making connections with the folks around you who are farming, baking, raising chickens or feeding goats. The more fully flavorful your basic ingredients are, the less you have to do to them (always a plus). A truly sublime summer tomato needs no truffle oil (a completely overrated and overused condiment, by the way, smelling to me like a skunk's armpit). And most importantly, you can't ravish your sweetheart up against the kitchen counter if she's going to be knocking her head against the stand mixer or the six different jars of imported salt along the way.

To have a welcoming kitchen (and enough cash in hand to treat your lover to champagne and smoked salmon as necessary), keep your cooking space uncluttered. Don't buy anything that serves only one purpose, especially if it's very large and bulky—although an exception must be made for salad spinners, one of the great inventions of the 20th century. And don't buy silly condiments, no matter how cute the jar. Cabernet-cranberry-horseradish mustard, lime and green peppercorn aioli, blueberry teriyaki sauce: no, no, no.

Equipment

If you haven't already gotten married (or domestic-partnered or civil-unioned) and stocked your kitchen accordingly at your friends' and families' expense, thrift stores and garage sales are your friends. Spend your money on a few good, heavy knives and a couple of heavy, high-quality sauté pans and saucepans. Cheap aluminum should be avoided, as should any very lightweight, flimsy-seeming pots and pans. Big-ticket items, like food processors and stand mixers, are only worth the splurge if you can swear on a bible that you'll be putting them to good use every week. I also feel strongly that a plastic-free kitchen is a happier and greener place to cook. Glass, wood, and ceramics last longer, look and work better, and don't seem to clutter up spaces nearly as much as plastic stuff does.

Baking items A muffin pan, a couple of round metal cake pans, a square metal or glass brownie pan, a pie plate (metal, glass, or ceramic), and a couple of (preferably heavy-gauge, unwarped) cookie sheets are the basics. Buy them once, and you won't have to keep running out for the crumply, disposable foil versions. They can also be used for multiple savory purposes: quiche, lasagna, casseroles. A bundt pan—a deep, doughnut-shaped round pan with a hole in the middle—is also more useful that you might think, especially for coffee cakes and carrot cake. Also, any kind of layer cake can be made in a bundt pan and then simply glazed or dusted with powdered sugar, meaning no fussing around with gobs of icing.

Even if, as a rule, you don't bake, you never know when you're going to end up with someone in your bed who really deserves a batch of homemade muffins in the morning. How far can a batch of fresh-from-the-oven double-chocolate mint cookies get you? Well, you'll never know unless you have a cookie sheet on which to bake them.

Also, have a decent toaster. Yes, you can toast under the broiler, but if you're like me, you'll stick the bread down there, move on to making the coffee and thus completely space out until your would-be toast is charcoal black. A toaster is a cheap and friendly alternative to flames shooting from the bottom of the oven. Plus, if you're entertaining picky Virgos, you don't want them getting all antsy about making toast on top of last night's (or last month's) broiled-chicken grease. Toaster ovens are more versatile (since you can make toasted cheese and tuna melts in them, and even bake cookies in a pinch) but they also take up more space, and take longer to make regular toast than your average two-slot job.

Cast Iron The frugal or space-starved cook's best friend. Cast iron skillets and Dutch ovens are cheap, wildly unglamorous, and cannot be improved, except for the fairly recent invention of pre-seasoning, which makes them ready to cook with right off the shelf. They move easily from stovetop to oven, and are nearly impossible to destroy. In one, you can fry chicken, push around a mess of vegetables, sizzle up eggs and sausages, roast a chicken or bake a batch of cornbread. I use mine in lieu of a roasting pan all the time, and while you couldn't roast a turkey or a big standing rib roast, for smaller jobs—a roast chicken, a pork tenderloin—it's perfect. Rust is cast iron's only enemy, and you can keep that at bay by gently scrubbing your pan out after using, drying it thoroughly over low heat, and swabbing a paper towel doused in vegetable oil over the cooking surface before you put it away.

Enameled Cast Iron The only thing better than cast iron is enameled cast iron. Not for everything; straight-up cast iron is still best for frying, baking, and roasting. But take a heavy, high-quality cast iron casserole or Dutch oven, coat it in thick, chip-resistant enamel, and you have the best cooking vessel for soups, stews, and braises that I've ever come across. The enamel keeps food from sticking, while the heavy cast iron distributes heat evenly and resists hot spots. Enamel is also non-reactive, which means you can cook tomatoes, wine, and other acidic things without worrying about the weird tang that can sometimes result when these things are cooked in cast iron.

The only drawbacks? It's heavy to lift, and the most durable, top-quality stuff, like Le Crueset, costs the earth, although you can often find it on sale online and at cookware outlets. The justification? It comes with a lifetime guarantee, and as long as you don't leave it empty over high heat (which can crack the enamel), nothing will go wrong with it for many, many years. Don't confuse something like Le Crueset with the thin, flimsy enamel pots and pans (usually white or speckled blue, with a black rim) available in your average hardware store. These can be handy for boiling eggs or heating up soup (or taking on camping trips), but they will burn, blacken, and chip in short order.

Knives Three knives will get you through most cooking jobs: a good-quality chef's knife, a small paring knife, and a serrated knife for slicing bread and tomatoes. Once you get the hang of a large, heavy knife, you'll find it can be used for loads of tasks, and is much more efficient than a shorter knife. That said, the knife I probably use the most in my kitchen is a smallish, stubby knife with a wide rubber handle, something like a fattened-up paring knife. Biggish tasks, like cutting up meat, chopping onions, or dicing a lot of vegetables require the chef's knife, absolutely. For the little jobs, you'll find the knife that your hand loves. Most importantly, keep these knives sharp. Get a steel or stone and learn how to use it, or get them professionally sharpened every few months. Dull knives are a drag, quite literally. A sharp knife is a safe knife, since you need less pressure to get the cutting done.

Measuring cups and spoons Dry measuring cups, in metal or plastic, come in graduated sizes, usually quarter, third, half, and full cup. As the name implies, they are for measuring dry ingredients, like flour and sugar. To get an accurate measurement, dip the cup into the flour, fill it up, then sweep the excess off with the flat of a knife (or your finger, always easier to find) so the top is even and flat. Don't shake down the cup so you can fit more stuff in! The only exception is brown sugar, which should be packed in as if you're making a sand castle. Liquid measuring cups are clear glass or plastic, with the gradations marked on the side. With the cup on an even surface, pour your milk or whatever in and check the measurement at eye level. Teaspoon measures come in strung-together sets, usually of 1/4 tsp, 1/2 tsp, 1 tsp, and 1 tbsp. 3 teaspoons make 1 tablespoon, a useful equation to know if you're doubling or tripling a recipe.

Microplane grater If there was one cooking implement that I would shill for on late-night TV, it would be the Microplane. Now available in various shapes, sizes, and grating levels, the Microplane is just a very sharp, finely-holed file with a long rounded handle. It stays wicked sharp, is a breeze to clean, and grates just about anything quickly and efficiently, with next to no waste. Once you use one, I promise you too will get all evangelical about it. I still use my big box grater for carrots, potatoes, and semi-firm cheese like cheddar and mozzarella, but for citrus peels, ginger, and hard cheese, the Microplane is it.

Ramekin A little obscure, but actually just a chichi sounding name for any round, ovenproof china dish, usually about 2 inches deep and 4 inches across. They aren't expensive, and they can do multiple duties around the house. Whether you fill them with olives, bake individual custards, cakes, or soufflés in them, or use them for dipping sauces, just get a few of these small ovenproof baking dishes, stack them up in a corner, and you'll be glad you did.

Things that Purée For some reason, people love to give me immersion blenders, also known as stick blenders—those things that look like vampire-fanged Hitachi Magic Wands. Maybe it's the visual of a vibrator with whirling teeth, but I've never warmed up to these, and despite their ease of use, I've never gotten a really smooth, consistent texture with one. So I wrap them up and pass them on instead, and keep using my old, cheap but reliable blender to purée soups, froth up smoothies and milkshakes, and make mayonnaise and hummus. As mentioned before, if you have to buy an appliance, go for the one that can multi-task without mess. One trick: if your blender comes with a removable little moon-roof in the center of the lid, always remove it when puréeing hot stuff, holding a towel over the opening if you think boiling gunk might splash out. This lets steam escape while you're puréeing, steam that might otherwise build up and shoot the whole lid (and all the whirling liquid below) up to the ceiling.

Ingredients

E very cook has a secret arsenal, a few absolutely necessary, alchemical ingredients that will transform, say, a humble roasted beet into a gorgeous tart-sweet salad (see pomegranate molasses, below). Lavender salt? Vanilla sugar? Mango chutney? Treasure your favorites instead of running after every new spice rub, barbecue sauce, or kinky mustard on the market. Too many cooks are condiment sluts (yes, Gemini and Aquarius, this means you), their refrigerator doors lined with murky, once-opened one-night stands. What you really need is a small assortment of high-quality, straightforward stuff: hot sauce (Tabasco, Crystal, or the sublime Asian Sriracha, or all three for you red-hot fire signs); soy sauce; Thai or Vietnamese-style fish sauce; Dijon mustard; olive oil; toasted sesame oil; red-wine vinegar; honey; natural peanut butter; a basic chutney; and a few good jams or jellies. These, at least, are my staples. Yours, depending on your favorite cuisines, may vary (hoisin sauce? Tahini? Harissa? Pickle relish?), but these basics will get you through most of the recipes in this book.

As for basic baking items—flour, sugar, baking powder and soda, cocoa, cinnamon, etc.—everyone should have these on hand, even if they don't bake. Why? Because when a pie-baking Libra hottie finds her way to your kitchen and wants to bake her extra-special coconut cream pie for you, well, what then? While she may bring her own coconut, she's going to assume that you'll at least have a bag of flour on hand (and a pie plate—see Equipment). And speaking from experience, everyone's a sucker for homemade baked goods, and they're much easier to make than you think.

Oh, and the most important thing? DON'T STORE YOUR INGREDIENTS OVER THE STOVE. This means spices and oils especially, all of which fade out and/or go rancid much, much faster in the face of heat and moisture. Salt, as a mineral, won't be affected, but everything else is going to lose flavor rapidly. Take down that little stove-side spice rack and find a nice nearby cabinet or drawer that stays comparatively dry, cool, and pest-free. And while you're at it, sniff and taste those spices and oils, chucking anything that doesn't smell like something you'd like to eat.

Baking powder The first thing to know about baking powder is that it doesn't last forever. It's a chemical— actually, an interacting combination of chemicals: one acidic, one basic, plus cornstarch to keep everything dry—and once it's dead, it will leave your muffins flat as pancakes. Unless you're a frequent baker, that can was bought four boyfriends ago and you should chuck it (it's cheap) and buy a fresh one. (There's an expiration date on the bottom; count on it working for about a year after opening.) I prefer non-aluminum brands, such as Rumson; they seem to have less of that weird metallic aftertaste that baking powder can sometimes impart. You can also mix up your own baking powder by mixing 2 parts cream of tartar with 1 part baking soda. Why should you know this? Just for that occasional late-night cake craving, when you've run out of baking powder but still have a mostly-untouched jar of cream of tartar in the spice rack. Why cream of tartar? Well, remember high school chemistry? Add an acid to a base, and you'll get a fun and dramatic chemical reaction. Cream of tartar is tartaric acid, and it will interact with the "base" of baking soda (sodium bicarbonate) to produce a fizz that will lighten your cake.

Baking soda Same as above. To check if it's still alive, dump a little in the sink and splash on some water. If it fizzes, it'll work; if not, use it to clean the sink and get a fresh box to use for cooking. Also, if you keep a box in the fridge to soak up smells, keep a fresh box in the pantry for baking.

Flour All-purpose unbleached flour is just fine for the recipes in this book. Look for *unbleached* flour—it has a little more life in it, not having been chemically bleached to bone-whiteness, and anyway, who needs to ingest more creepy chemicals? Whole-wheat pastry flour, if you can find it (bulk bins at a health-food store are a good place to look), can be substituted for regular white flour most of the time; it will give you a slightly denser, heavier product with a grainier texture and a nutty, more earthy flavor.

Cheese

Assuming you already know the cheeses you like, here are a few used in this book:

Cheddar Of course, you've had cheddar. But if you love even the waxy orange blocks from the supermarket, go seek out the good stuff. Cut from huge wheels in a fancy cheese shop, British cheddars are flaky, dense, slightly salty, and heavenly. Vermont's Grafton cheddar is also worth seeking out, as are any well-aged Wisconsin cheddars.

Chevre (fresh goat cheese). Soft, crumbly, and moist with a very mild, creamy but discernable goaty flavor. Beloved by some, derided by others. Very nice crumbled over salads or used in sandwiches or bruschetta. As a fresh cheese, chevre doesn't have that long of a shelf life in the fridge. Keep it tightly wrapped, and once opened, use within a couple of weeks.

Feta White, salty, and lovely, kept moist in a bath of brine. Can be made from sheep, goat, or cow's milk; sheep is most expensive but has a fantastic flavor beloved by those who like their cheese on the earthy/gamey side.

Parmesan Real parmesan comes from Italian cows, and not any Italian cows, but Italian cows raised on pasture in a specific part of Reggio-Emilia, near Parma. Hence its proper name, Parmigiano-Reggiano. Real parmesan comes in enormous wheels with the name inked on the hard, waxy rind. It should be dense and slightly crystalline, with a salty bite and a mouth-watering savoriness. A big hunk is expensive, but kept wrapped tightly in wax paper in the refrigerator, it lasts for a very long time, and it doesn't take much to add a lot of flavor to pastas, savory custards, egg dishes, and more. Yes, the pre-grated stuff is easier and useful to have on hand. Most good grocery stores or cheese shops sell plastic tubs full of freshly grated real parmesan, or a mix of parmesan and romano cheeses. These last an equally long time and are free of all the scary additives and general ickiness that goes into prefab "cheese food" like the salty sand sold in those shiny, nasty green cans.

Chocolate

Chocolate Unsweetened, or baking, chocolate, is just that: straight up chocolate, used for baking, with no added sugar. (Not to be confused with Baker's German Sweet Chocolate, a semi-sweet brand.) Bittersweet and semi-sweet chocolate both have sugar added, and can be eaten plain and used for baking. Many chocolates now label themselves by their percentage of cocoa solids; the higher the percentage, the more intense (and less sweet) the chocolate. Taste around and find your favorite; a typical bittersweet chocolate will have between 65% and 72% cocoa solids. Lindt, Scharffenberger, Valhrona, Guittard, Callebaut, and Ghirardelli all make high-quality bittersweet and semi-sweet bars.

Cocoa Powder Not to be confused with cocoa mix, unsweetened cocoa powder is a soft, dark brown, very bitter powder that has a deep, chocolately fragrance. For high-octane chocolate flavor, skip the typical cartons of Nestle and Hershey. Instead, try the cocoa powders made by Ghirardelli, Droste, Scharffenberger, or Valhrona.

Once you've got a box of cocoa around, you can start making real hot cocoa, which is a million times yummier than the sugary brown water made from a mix (or at the ice rink). For one cup, stir 1 heaping tbsp cocoa, 2 tsp brown or white sugar (or to taste), and 2 tbsp milk in a cup to form a paste. (This will keep the cocoa from clumping up in the larger amount of milk.) In a small pot, heat 1 cup of milk until just steaming. Scrape in the cocoa paste and whisk or stir until it's nice and hot. Add a few drops of vanilla extract or a shot of peppermint schnapps. Top with whipped cream or marshmallows.

Sauce and Seasoning

Olive oil The reason Italians have such gorgeous skin and hair. Olive oil is luscious and good for you, but only if you haven't let it get all old and rancid in the cabinet while you ran around with the Wesson (or, heaven forbid, that toxic-smelling spray-on Pam). Sniff it before use: it should have a clean, olive-y scent. If it smells old or cardboard-ish, chuck it, get a fresh bottle, and store the new one in the fridge if it won't be used much. It will solidify, but that's easily fixed: when needed, just stand the bottle in a bowl of hot water until it liquefies enough to use.

Fish sauce Available in Asian grocery stores, sometimes in the Asian-condiments section of well-stocked supermarkets, and usually imported from Thailand or Vietnam. It is what it says: the runoff from sun-cured, salted small fish, mostly anchovies. Closely related to *garum*, a popular condiment in ancient Roman times, now a good Scrabble word. It is clear, amber to dark brown, with a pungent odor. Its taste isn't exactly fishy, more just an essence of salty savoriness, a bit like soy sauce, but much milder and less brawny. Nothing you'd want to drink straight, but it has a magical ability to push up flavor and bring salty-sweet-sour-hot into balance. Inexpensive and very long-lasting.

Peanut butter Raised by high-minded but gastronomically adventurous Virgo/Capricorn parents (Mom made her own granola; Dad ferreted out good ethnic restaurants even in deepest suburbia), I grew up on all-natural peanut butter, the kind that had to have all its naturally separated oil painstakingly and sloppily mixed back in before using. This is still the case with all-natural peanut butter, and it's still just as messy a job. However, it's the only kind of peanut butter that actually tastes like peanuts, rather than super-sweet, trans-fatted goo. You don't want to use the sugary kids' stuff (Jif, Skippy, et al) for savory recipes, and frankly, if you value your teeth and your health, you don't want to eat it in sandwiches or on your celery sticks either. Almond, hazelnut or sunflower-seed butters offer a similar consistency with different flavors.

Pepper Pre-ground black pepper is completely useless. Get a pepper grinder, fill it up with whole peppercorns, and grind as needed. Once ground, pepper loses its bite rapidly, so whenever possible, add it just before serving.

Pomegranate molasses Tangy, fruity heaven, this Middle Eastern condiment is just pomegranate juice boiled down to the consistency of maple syrup. Divine with beets, figs, and oranges, and an all-around nifty thing to have around the house. Look for it at Middle Eastern or specialty grocery stores.

Salt Sea salt has a clear, pure taste that is recommended for all the recipes in this book. A fine-grain, inexpensive sea salt can be your standard go-to. Keep it handy so you can dip into it at will, but don't leave it in a place (like near the sink) where the bottom of the container can get wet, since left that way, the whole container will eventually solidify into a salty rock. Coarse, flaky sea salt, like the English Malden salt or French fleur de sel, is nice to have on hand for sprinkling over finished dishes like bruschetta, salads, and grilled meats. You can keep going with Hawaiian pink salt, Celtic gray salt, lavender salt, truffle salt... just keep in mind the mantra about keeping your kitchen clutter at a minimum.

Sugar Granulated sugar is your basic white stuff. You can feel slightly more—what? natural? Birkenstocky?—by using raw sugar, which comes in coarser, unbleached pale amber crystals. Brown sugar, usually made by dosing white sugar with molasses, is moist and crumbly, and as mentioned above, should always be packed in the cup when measuring. (Fuller-flavored, less processed brown sugars are sold in fancy shops as muscavado or demarara sugars.) Powdered, or confectioner's, sugar is very fine and powdery, with a little cornstarch mixed in. It should always be sifted before using, to thwart its tendency to clump.

Toasted sesame oil As the original *Moosewood Cookbook* once said, this is the stuff that will make you glad to have a nose. Just a little added as a finishing condiment will give a lavishly nutty, unctuous whiff to all kinds of Asian-inspired foods. Sold in smallish bottles, it's deep amber-colored, intensely aromatic and viscous. Not to be confused with regular raw sesame oil, which is clear, yellow, and can be used for frying and other typical oily things.

The Signs

Aries

March 21-April 19

Symbol: Ram

Ruler: Mars

Element: Fire

Quality: Cardinal

Ram's Horns and Lamb's Ears

Spring comes in with a blast on the back of Aries the ram. As the first sign of the zodiac, Aries is driven by a passionate resolve to stay at the head of the pack. Direct, decisive, and full of energy, competitive Arians are most fully engaged when they're in combat mano-a-mano. With Mars, the god of war, as their ruling planet, Aries thrives on a challenge. Not just a challenge, actually: they love to skirt the rules on their way to success. They're not quite outlaws, but they're definitely mavericks who use their intelligence, street smarts, and persistence to achieve their goals.

To romance an Aries, give them a few dragons to slay, or not-quite-ex's to vanquish. Aries like to flirt, and they especially like to imagine that their personal (and physical) charm can overcome all obstacles tossed in their way. Don't just hand over your business card to an Aries; give them a few hints, then let them track you down.

Stalkerish? No way! Aries are too social, and too invested in their own personal sense of cool, to be freaky like that. Then again, my Aries sister did once track down a guy she'd met in a hotel hot tub, knowing only his first name and the fact that he taught high-school math and played rugby nearby, long before Google made this sort of thing way too easy. The result? He was thrilled to get the *Magnum P.I.* treatment from a smart, marathon-running babe (whom he'd already seen in a bikini) and they dated for the following year.

And speaking of marathons, rough and tumble is the way to the Aries' heart when it comes to romancing. Skip the long walks on the beach and tinkly pianos in the candlelight. Instead, take your Aries man or woman rock-climbing, rafting, or just out for a little Bond-style parkeur around the city. These work-hard, play-hard rams pair best with partners who can hang tough in the face of their fiery determination. Don't forget the Band-Aids, though: in their damn-the-torpedoes haste, they can end up bumped, bruised, and knocked around. It's all in a day's fun, though—a ram never whines. Complains, maybe—mostly about others' incompetence or lack of ambition—but whines, no.

Like Leo and Sagittarius (their fellow fire signs), Aries loves an audience. This can translate into a desire to prove themselves and show off for you (fun) and a need to have lots of admirers standing around clapping while they do so (not so fun, if the clappers turn into groupies). Mavericks that they are, Aries take attention, especially amorous attention, as their due, which doesn't always make them the most faithful of partners. Actually, that's not exactly true: sure, they like to play around, or at least get a lot of flirtatious Scoobie snacks at parties, but they also depend on the stability of a longtime partner for emotional grounding and true understanding. So if you can trust that your Aries sweetie will always come home to you, sit back and enjoy the show.

Like a ram skittering up a steep mountainside, Aries are highly social and adaptable and rarely lose their footing. They can chat up just about anyone, and have no fear of broaching a crowded party or unfamiliar setting—in fact, like Libra, their opposite sun-sign sisters, these are party people who thrive on festivity. Aries want to be where the action is, which make hip, noisy restaurants and the latest go-to lounges these rams' natural habitat.

To get them to focus on you, start the night at a favorite bar, bring the temperature up with some very directed flirtation, then bring them home for the real meat of the night.

These menus are arranged for do-ahead ease that makes getting dinner on the table a snap—which means less chance for work-hard, play-hard Aries to get tweeted and text-messaged out to another party. Tender lamb, spring greens, artichokes, sharp sheep's milk feta: these are big, uncomplicated flavors built to satisfy a generous and unfussy appetite.

You can make this menu any time, of course, using frozen strawberries for the vinaigrette and a mixture of chopped green onions and regular garlic for the flan. But this menu is particularly vibrant made with fresh spring produce, from the sweetest strawberries and the most tender baby lettuces to the most succulent fresh asparagus. If you can find a source of fresh local lamb (check farmers' markets in your area, or ask at a good butcher shop or specialty food store), you'll be well on the way to making your Aries sweetheart swoon.

Menu

Asparagus & Green Garlic Flan
Greek Lamb Stew with Artichokes & Feta Cheese
or Gicante Bean Casserole with Tomato & Feta Cheese
Baby Greens with Strawberry Vinaigrette
Meyer Lemon Bars

Asparagus & Green Garlic Flan

Green, or spring, garlic shows up at farmers' markets in springtime, and is nothing fancier than immature garlic, harvested before the stalks dry out and the heads form distinct, papery-wrapped cloves. Green at the top, white at the bottom, green garlic stalks look like skinny, fat-bottomed leeks. Scrape them lightly with a fingernail and you'll get a heady whiff of garlic—milder than the mature clove, but definitely more pungent than the average leek or scallion. To perfume this silky-rich custard, use the white part and about a third of the pale green stalk. And please use real Parmesan, not the prefab salty sand sold in shiny green cans.

2 tbsp butter
1/2 lb asparagus
2 or 3 stalks of green garlic, white and pale green parts only
1 tbsp finely chopped fresh chives, parsley, chervil, or tarragon
1/2 tsp salt
black pepper

pinch of freshly grated nutmeg
2 large eggs
2/3 cup whole milk
2 tbsp half-and-half or heavy cream (optional)
3 tbsp freshly grated parmesan

Preheat oven to 325°F. Butter 4 ramekins, custard cups, or ovenproof glass baking dishes.

Snap off woody ends of asparagus and discard. Fill a wide skillet with about 1/2 inch of water. Bring to a boil, add asparagus, and simmer until just tender. Drain in a colander, running cold water over the asparagus to cool. Slice asparagus stalks very finely, cutting tips in half lengthwise. In the same skillet, melt remaining butter and sauté green garlic until just softened, 2 to 3 minutes. Remove from heat and add asparagus, herbs, salt, pepper, and nutmeg.

In a small bowl, whisk together eggs, milk, cream (if using), salt, pepper, and nutmeg. Stir in asparagus mixture and grated cheese. Divide between ramekins. Set ramekins in a baking dish and set in the oven. Pour hot water in the baking dish to come up halfway around ramekins. Bake for 20 minutes, or until custards are set. Remove and let cool for 5 minutes before serving. Try unmolding them if you're feeling glamorous (and lucky). Run a butter knife down the edges of each dish to loosening the flan. Hold a plate tightly against the top of the flan, flip over and give a sharp shake. Remove ramekin, and voila! The flan should be standing up, jiggly and proud, on the dish.

Greek Lamb Stew with Artichokes & Feta Cheese

This stew tastes even better if made the day before serving. If you plan to make it ahead of time, leave out the feta and parsley. Let it cool to room temperature, then refrigerate. Before serving, remove any fat that has risen to the surface, and reheat gently. Add feta and parsley just before serving, and accompany it with rice spritzed with lemon juice or a loaf of crusty sesame-seed bread.

3-4 tbsp olive oil
1 medium yellow onion, peeled and finely chopped
1 1/2 lbs stewing lamb, cut into bite-sized chunks
salt and pepper
3 tbsp flour
2 sprigs of fresh rosemary, thyme or oregano, or 1/2 tsp of dried
2 bay leaves, fresh if possible

1/2 cup white wine
1 cup crushed tomatoes, or chopped tomatoes with juice
1 cup water
1 tbsp capers
1 14-oz can artichoke hearts, drained and rinsed, cut into quarters
6 oz feta cheese, broken into large chunks
2-3 tbsp chopped fresh parsley

Preheat oven to 300°F. Sprinkle lamb with salt and pepper. Spread flour on a plate. Roll lamb cubes around in the flour. Heat up 2 tablespoons olive oil in a heavy Dutch oven or ovenproof casserole. Shake off excess flour from meat, then add meat to the hot oil. (You'll probably need to do this in a couple of batches.) Let the meat sizzle for a few minutes, then turn over to brown on both sides. As lamb is browned, remove to a bowl and set aside. Add more oil as necessary.

When all the lamb is browned and removed from the pan, add onion. Cook, stirring, over medium heat until onion is soft and golden. Add the garlic and herb sprigs. Cook, stirring, for 1 minute. Add wine and cook for a minute or two, stirring and scraping to loosen browned bits from the bottom of the pan. Add meat, tomatoes, and water and bring to a gentle simmer.

Cover pan and slide into preheated oven. Let cook, covered, for 1 1/2 hours. Add capers and quartered artichoke hearts. Cook for another 20 minutes, or until meat is very tender and sauce has thickened (remove cover for the last 15 minutes if sauce seems thin).

Stir in feta cheese. Taste for seasoning. Sprinkle with chopped parsley and serve.

Gigante Bean Casserole with Tomato & Feta Cheese

This is the Greek Ram's comfort food: creamy beans bathed in garlicky tomato sauce, with chunks of feta and a crunch of browned breadcrumbs on top. This makes a good meatless entree, or a sturdy side dish with fish or chicken. Look for gigante beans (which really are that big; think lima beans on steroids) in Greek or Middle Eastern specialty stores. Or just substitute the biggest dried white beans you can find, adjusting the boiling time accordingly.

1/2 cup chopped flat-leaf parsley
1/4 cup chopped fresh dill
1/2 cup tomato sauce
1/4 tsp smoked paprika (optional)
1/2 cup crumbled feta
1/3 cup coarse, homemade breadcrumbs

1/2 lb dried gigante, lima, or cannelini beans
1 carrot, peeled and diced
1 celery stick, diced
1 large onion, thinly sliced
2 cloves garlic, peeled and smashed
1/4 cup olive oil
1 bay leaf

Place the beans in a large pot. Cover with water. Bring to a boil, simmer for 2 minutes and drain, rinsing off any froth.

Return beans to the pot, adding carrot, celery, bay leaves and garlic. Cover with water. Bring to a boil, reduce heat, and cook, barely simmering, for 30-45 minutes, until beans are tender. Remove from heat. Drain beans and vegetables, reserving liquid and discarding bay leaves.

Preheat oven to 375°F. In a large skillet, heat olive oil over medium heat. Add onions and sauté, stirring frequently, until softened and translucent, 8-10 minutes. Stir in the tomato sauce, paprika, parsley and dill.

Spread beans and vegetables in an 8" x 8" baking dish. Stir in tomato mixture. Sprinkle with crumbled feta, pressing feta down into beans. If mixture looks dry, add reserved bean liquid as necessary so mixture is moist and sludgy but not soupy.

Bake for 30 minutes, adding a little more liquid as needed if mixture looks dry. Top with breadcrumbs and let bake another 10-15 minutes, until breadcrumbs are crisp and golden. Serve hot or at room temperature.

Baby Greens with Strawberry Vinaigrette

Choose a mixture of fresh spring greens, including mache (also known as lamb's lettuce), arugula, frisee, spinach, and various young lettuces. The amount depends on how much salad the two of you like to eat.

mixed greens
a pint of strawberries
a handful of sliced almonds
mild oil, such as grapeseed or a mixture of canola and olive oils
salt and freshly ground pepper to taste

Rinse and dry greens. In a small skillet over medium heat, dry-toast the sliced almonds, stirring constantly, until they are just golden and slightly browned at the edges. Remove from heat and set aside. Slice up about two-thirds of the strawberries and set aside. In a blender or mini-chopper, purée remaining strawberries, oil, salt and pepper. Taste for seasoning. Just before serving, toss greens with sliced strawberries and half the dressing. Add additional dressing as needed. Top with toasted almonds.

Meyer Lemon Bars

Oh, Meyer lemons. Truly a food of the gods, and reason enough to decamp for sunny California, wherever you may live. The Meyer lemon is half mandarin orange, half lemon, and has a thin, glovelike, incredibly fragrant skin wrapped around a sweet-tart, deep golden pulp. They're much more fragile than a regular lemon, which means they're scarce and pricey away from the West Coast, where they're commonly grown as a garden tree. But your Aries sweetie will appreciate the trouble you've gone to to get them (even more so if you scavenged or sweet-talked them out of a stranger's backyard), and their flavor makes these lemon bars extra-delish. However, they'll be very, very good even made with regular lemons.

Crust:
1 cup all-purpose flour
1/2 cup melted butter (1 stick, or 8 tbsp)
1/2 cup powdered sugar

Filling:
1/2 cup granulated sugar
1/2 tsp baking powder
2 eggs
6 tbsp lemon juice (2 to 3 lemons)
1 tbsp finely grated lemon zest
powdered sugar

Preheat oven to 350°F. Grease an 8" x 8" pan. Sift together flour and sugar (a fine-mesh strainer works just fine if you don't have a sifter). Mix in melted butter until you have a smooth dough. Pat into pan.
Bake for 20 minutes until lightly colored.

Sift or whisk sugar and baking powder together. Beat eggs lightly, then add to sugar along with the lemon juice and zest. Mix thoroughly. Pour over warm crust and return to oven for 20-25 minutes. Let cool to room temperature, then sift a drift of powdered sugar over top. If not serving within a few hours, cut into bars, cover, and refrigerate.

Taurus
April 20-May 20

Symbol: Bull

Quality: Fixed

Ruler: Venus

Element: Earth

Sexy Beast

Mmmm, yummy. That's the Taurus approach to life, also translated as bigger, faster, deeper, more. These bulls are prodigious in their appetites, but they're also earthbound homebodies, Venus-ruled domestic sensualists who adore their Egyptian cotton sheets, their fine wines, their big-screen TVs, and spanking the fine bottom of their choice.

Like Libra, their partner in Venus, Taurus lives for love. Or at least some really good nooky, which for Taurus can often look like the same thing. A perfect weekend for Taurus would start with a snappy, dressy night out on Friday, then proceed to the bedroom and, with plenty of pauses for scented bubble baths and luscious finger foods from the best gourmet shop in town, stay there until Sunday night, when it's time to shake the crumbs from the sheets, pop in a DVD of *Gentleman Prefer Blondes* and call for an extra-large pizza with everything.

Or maybe that was just the way of one fabulous Taurus I knew, who loved to entertain a rotating crew of smart and very talented strippers at home. Even though home was a basement apartment with low ceilings and less-than-glam beige carpeting, the ladies kept coming back, because their lusty Taurus lover treated them all like queens. But Taurus's need for pampering (and instant gratification) leads them to the phone and takeout menus more often than to the stove. Which means they'll be extra-impressed, and happily wallowing in their element, if you take the time and effort to cook for them at home.

Don't be too fooled by the circus of the senses that can surround Taurus. Fixed and earthy, they are remarkably grounded and pragmatic when it comes to business and money matters, even if they sometimes aspire to status symbols beyond their means. Left to their own appetites, Taurus would order a shrimp cocktail to start, prime rib with eggplant parmigiana on the side, garlic bread and Caesar salad and why yes, profiteroles for dessert would be lovely, darlin'. A little exaggeration, for sure, but it's not a bad idea to guide the Taurean appetite towards vegetables—especially gut-healthy, probiotic preparations like kimchee and lacto-fermented sauerkrauts—to balance with their natural inclination towards meat and sweets.

Depending on how comfortable you are sharing the stage in the kitchen, you may want to get the cooking done before your sweetie shows up, because once they drift over to the stove, they're going to want to get their hands sticky. And you know what that means: larger, hotter, smokier, more, more. A little hot sauce becomes a LOT of hot sauce, a tablespoon of butter becomes an entire stick, a half-cup of wine turns into the whole bottle dumped into the soup. What you get is big taste, not balance, which, depending on your own sign, can be either lots of fun (bananas with the salmon? Sure, why not!) or utter tragedy (You. Have Just. Ruined. Our Dinner). Know yourself and cook ahead, or be prepared to charmingly overruled, even on your own turf.

With its broad, lusty flavors, this Korean barbecue should sate the Taurean palate without sending him or her into sleepy food overload. If you have access to an outdoor barbecue, get Taurus to man (or woman) the grill—always a favorite task for these heat seekers. And then, finish it all off with a happy, gooey ice cream sundae, slick and slippery with hot fudge sauce. Lick your fingers and see if he'll beg for the cherry on top.

Menu

Kalbi (Korean Short Ribs) or Spicy Tofu
Korean Glass Noodles (Chop Chae)
Sautéed Bok Choy
Kim Chee
Ice Cream Sundaes

Kalbi (Korean Short Ribs) or Spicy Tofu

Most of the recipes in this book are made to serve two generously. But somehow, the Taurus recipes just refused to be scaled down. Taurus's ruling characteristic is generosity, and the Taurus appetite is prodigious. So this makes plenty for dinner, midnight snacks, and lunch the next day.

1/2 cup soy sauce	2 tbsp honey
1/4 cup mirin (sweet Japanese rice wine) or sweet sherry	2 tbsp Asian (toasted) sesame oil
2 tbsp (packed) dark brown sugar	2 tbsp minced garlic
1/4 cup rice vinegar	2 large scallions (green onions), chopped
2 tbsp fresh grated ginger	1 tsp Asian chili sauce, such as Sriracha, or more to taste

2 lbs Korean-style beef short ribs, cut 1/3 to 1/2 inch thick across bones—or 1 lb firm tofu, cut into triangles
garnish: 2 large scallions (green onions), minced—and 1 tbsp sesame seeds
1 cup jasmine or basmati rice, optional

In a medium bowl whisk together all ingredients except the ribs or tofu. Pour off about a quarter of the mixture into a small bowl, cover and refrigerate. Pour the rest of the marinade into a heavy resealable plastic bag. Add ribs or tofu and seal bag. Double-check that bag is tightly sealed, then turn over several times to make sure ribs are thoroughly coated. Refrigerate for at least 2 and up to 8 hours, turning bag occasionally.

For the optional rice: About 20 to 50 minutes before serving, bring rice to a boil with 1 3/4 cups of water. Add a generous pinch of salt, cover pot tightly, and reduce heat to low. Let simmer for 12-15 minutes for white rice, 40 minutes for brown. Turn off the heat and let rice finish cooking in its own residual heat for at least 10 to 15 minutes.

Prepare grill (medium-high heat) or broiler. While grill is heating, remove small bowl of reserved marinade from the fridge. In a small saucepan over medium heat, simmer reserved marinade until syrupy and reduced by half. Set aside. Drain ribs and discard marinade in bag. Working in batches, grill or broil ribs until browned and cooked to medium-rare, about 3 minutes per side. If using tofu, grill until browned in stripes and heated through. Pile ribs or tofu on platter, drizzle with cooked marinade, and sprinkle with scallions and sesame seeds.

Korean Glass Noodles (Chop Chae)

Look in an Asian market for clear, slippery Korean potato-starch noodles. If you can't find them, substitute Vietnamese-style rice-stick or glass noodles instead.

2 tbsp sesame oil, or more as needed
2 medium carrots, peeled and julienned
1 large onion, peeled, thinly sliced and separated into rings
12 scallions, trimmed and chopped
2 cups chopped cooked spinach (sure, use the frozen stuff)
1 cup interesting mushrooms, sliced such as shiitake, cremini, and/or oyster

1 tbsp minced garlic
1/2 lb potato-starch noodles (available in Korean markets)
2 tbsp soy sauce
salt and pepper to taste
1/4 cup pine nuts, lightly toasted (optional)
2 tbsp sesame seeds

Bring a large pot of water to a boil. Put 1 tablespoon of the sesame seed oil into a skillet, and turn heat to medium high. Cook the carrots in the skillet, stirring occasionally, just until they lose their crunch, about 5 minutes. Scoop into a bowl.

Put the remaining sesame seed oil in the skillet, and add the onion; cook, stirring occasionally, until it begins to brown, about 5 minutes. Remove with a slotted spoon, and add to the bowl of carrots. Raise heat to high, and add the scallions. Cook, stirring, until they wilt, just 2 or 3 minutes. Add to carrots.

Add a little more oil if necessary, and stir-fry the spinach until hot, 3 to 5 minutes. Add to the meat mixture. Add the mushrooms and garlic, and cook, stirring occasionally, until they soften, about 5 minutes.

Add noodles to the boiling water, and turn off the heat. Noodles will be tender in about 5 minutes; drain. Add noodles and soy sauce to skillet, and cook, stirring occasionally, for about 5 minutes.

Toss noodles with vegetables in bowl to mix, adding more sesame oil or soy sauce to taste. Garnish with pine nuts and sesame seeds. Serve at room temperature.

Sautéed Bok Choy

The smaller the head, the tenderer the bok choy; look for what's often called "baby bok choy" for the sweetest, softest greens and fleshiest stems. If you can't find bok choy, try using thinly sliced Napa or Chinese cabbage. Count on one head of baby bok choy per person.

2-3 heads baby bok choy, separated
1 tbsp peanut or other neutral vegetable oil
2 cloves garlic, sliced
1-2 tsp roasted sesame oil, or to taste

Rinse bok choy leaves, but don't dry. Heat oil in a large skillet and add leaves. Cook, stirring, until stems have softened slightly, 1-2 minutes. Add garlic slices and cook for another 30-60 seconds, until leaves and stems are tender. Sprinkle with sesame oil to taste.

Kim Chee

This fiery condiment was named a national treasure by the Korean government and is Korea's answer to sauerkraut. Traditionally made from Napa cabbage (although there are as many variations as there are grandmas), with hot peppers, salt, and other flavorings, it's ubiquitous with every Korean meal. Sour, hot, and salty, it makes a vibrant palate-cleanser for the big flavors of this Taurus meal. As a naturally fermented food, it's also full of gut-healthy probiotics. Look for it in the refrigerated Asian-foods section of a well-stocked supermarket, or ask for it in an Asian market. Not to everyone's taste, but once you're hooked, it's hard to imagine any rich, spicy meal without it.

Ice Cream Sundaes

Who doesn't like a hot-fudge sundae? Taurus sure does, especially when it comes with whipped cream and yes, a cherry on top. Throw in a banana there too (potassium!) and you'll have a gooey treat to please even the fieriest bull. Normally, I'd scream and stamp on the side of beating up some real whipped cream, made with heavy cream, your arm, and a whisk or hand-held electric beater. But in certain situations, that whipped cream out of a can can be a lot of fun. If that's the road you take, just read the label and be sure you're buying as much real cream as possible, and don't waste your time on some ersatz "lite" junk. (When food companies take out the fat, they put in the high-fructose corn syrup, and this is as true for salad dressing and cookies as it is for whipped topping.)

ice cream, in fudge-compatible flavors	chopped nuts (optional)
bananas	whipped cream
hot fudge sauce (see below)	maraschino or fresh cherries

Hot Fudge Sauce

This makes more than you'll need, but then again, it comes in handy.

1 cup heavy cream	pinch salt
2 tbsp unsalted butter	1 oz bittersweet chocolate, chopped
1/4 cup light brown sugar	1/2 cup unsweetened cocoa powder
1/3 cup granulated sugar	1/2 tsp vanilla extract

In medium saucepan, combine cream, butter, sugars, and salt. Bring to a simmer over medium-low heat, stirring until sugar dissolves. Remove from heat. Add chocolate and cocoa mixture and let stand for a minute or two.

Return pan to low heat, and whisk vigorously until smooth and glossy, about 30 seconds. Remove from heat and stir in vanilla. Serve warm. To reheat, warm in a small saucepan over low heat, stirring constantly. Do not boil.

For the sundae, slice banana lengthwise. Nestle it in a sundae dish or boat. Top with two scoops of ice cream. Drizzle lavishly with hot fudge sauce. Top with nuts, whipped cream, and cherry.

Gemini

May 21–June 20

Symbol: Twins   Element: Air
Ruler: Mercury   Quality: Mutable (last sign of spring)

Paradise in the South Seas

Lucky, lucky Gemini. These twins can talk their way into—or out of—any situation. Want to go backstage, wriggle out of a speeding ticket, get the number of that cute guy behind the bar? Enlist the help of a Gemini—they are the zodiac's born wingmen, happy to put their many charms to work for their pals. Don't get in their way when they're making their own moves, however; their glitter can outshine any mere mortal in the vicinity.

The slippery, changeable nature of Geminis often gets them lumped in with highly emotional signs like Pisces and Cancer. Not so fast! Unlike those fluid water signs, Gemini has a highly rational, logical aspect (bred from their ruling planet Mercury, which represents the power of the mind) that allows them to take a step back from their feelings. Even in the midst of powerful passions, independent-minded Gemini can analyze a romantic situation with disconcertingly cool rationality. Imaginative and inquisitive, Geminis are seekers and drawn to spirituality, self-actualization, even the occult, but they bring a balance of emotion and logic even to their pursuit of personal growth. They love to follow a path and will throw themselves whole-heartedly into whatever intrigues them, even if they're off onto a new track in a few months (or days, since Gemini's moods, and whims, can change by the hour).

They also enjoy testing their willpower and capacity for discipline, as long as it doesn't take too much of the pleasure out of daily life. Holistic medicine, feng shui, meditation, aryuveda, the Atkins diet—Gemini probably has given all of these a whirl at one point or another. At any given moment they're probably following some quirky dietary regime— going raw, juice-cleansing, eating for their blood type—but their happily mutable nature means they can usually be coaxed out of any dogmatic principle if it tastes good enough.

Have we made Geminis sound like moody, crystal-wearing, dreamcatcher-dangling New Age types? They have that potential, sure. But thankfully, for all their brainy spirituality, they're also very naughty monkeys. Mercury, their ruling planet, may be connected with mental energy, but it's also named for the messenger and trickster of the gods.

Geminis are happiest when they're generating some entertaining trouble. As natural flirts with libidinous energy in abundance, they like to stir up a little jealousy in their partners, just to keep the home fires burning a little hotter. For the long haul, they need an even-tempered sweetheart who can appreciate the shimmer when they spread their shine around. But you'd better be ready to process—Geminis approach relationships with as much verve as they do other crazes, and they need a partner willing to talk and talk... and talk... about needs, goals, and what it all means. Because they're such charmers, they fear being mistaken for lightweights in the brain department, so it's crucial to make them feel appreciated for their intellects as much as for their smokin' bods.

Ah, yes! Those lips, those eyes, those pecs… These saucy parrots and fluttering butterflies need sea, sun, and sand to thrive. Think Hawaii, the Caribbean, Bali, Indonesia, Tahiti, and Fiji—then light the tiki torches and bring out the orchids and sarongs when you're ready to woo.

Gemini has a tendency to balance all that changeability with soothing comfort foods, whether it's a platter of cheese grits and ribs, or mashed potatoes right out of the pot. But what's healthier for them—and livelier for you—are light, tangy foods in a sweet-tangy-salty balance, with just a little fried on the side. After all, you don't want your sparkly charmer laid out snoozing in a food coma. Thai and Vietnamese flavors will satisfy their wanderlust and keep their fickle palates entertained. As you might expect, Geminis aren't big on following recipes. They'll browse cookbooks for ideas, then follow their own moods, letting their flights of fancy lead them through the supermarket and out into the kitchen. So if you want to cook together, be flexible, and let Gemini's creativity flow.

Menu

Thai-Style Summer Rolls
Seared Tuna with Avocado-Mango Salsa
Bangkok Melon Salad
Yam Balls
Pineapple Coconut Custards

Thai-Style Summer Rolls

Cool, clear, and crunchy, these summer rolls are way more delicious than the ones you'll get in almost any Thai restaurant. Why? Because they're filled to bursting with super crunchy shredded veggies and flavor-soaked cellophane noodles. Did this recipe come from some little beachside snack shack on Koh Samui? Um, no. Instead, you can thank Jane Tucker, backstage caterer for the many fabulous performers that have played at The Auditorium in downtown Eureka Springs, Arkansas. Jane also helps run the Writers' Colony at Dairy Hollow, a fantastic retreat for creative types of all stripes, including cookbook writers.

Filling:
2 oz cellophane (mung bean) noodles, thin rice-stick noodles, or rice vermicelli; 1 1/2 cups (total) mixed shredded raw carrot, red cabbage, bok choy, or Chinese (napa) cabbage; 1 cup fresh bean sprouts; 1/2 cup minced fresh cilantro; 2 green onions (scallions), finely chopped; 1 8-oz can water chestnuts, drained, rinsed, and slivered (optional); 1/2 lb firm tofu, cubed; 1 clove garlic, minced

Dressing:
2 tbsp rice vinegar; 2 tbsp minced or grated fresh ginger; 1 tbsp roasted Asian sesame oil;
1 tbsp soy sauce; 1/2 tsp hot sauce, such as Srichica (optional)

Wrapping:
8 green lettuce leaves, any heavy center ribs removed; 1 avocado (peeled, pitted, and sliced);
mint leaves; Thai basil leaves; 8 extra-thin rice paper rounds

Dipping Sauce:
juice of 1 lime; 1 tbsp rice vinegar; 2 tsp soy sauce; 1 tsp brown sugar (or to taste); 1 tsp grated fresh ginger;
leaves of 2 sprigs fresh cilantro, minced; 4 or 5 roasted peanuts, finely chopped; 1 green onion (scallion), thinly sliced

Bring 4 cups water to a boil. Add cellophane noodles. Boil for 1 minute, then remove pot from heat and let stand for 5 minutes. Drain noodles. If using rice noodles, soak in hot water for 15 minutes until softened. Bring a separate pot of water to a boil, add noodles and boil for 1 minute. Drain and rinse.

Mix noodles with remaining filling ingredients. In a small bowl, whisk together dressing ingredients. Pour dressing over filling mixture, tossing well.

Set up lettuce leaves, avocado slices, mint, and basil leaves. Lay out a clean tea towel in front of you. Dip rice paper round into a shallow bowl of warm water until slightly softened but still partially stiff. This will only take 10-20 seconds, and it's better to err on the side of stiffness. Lay rice paper round on towel. Place lettuce leaf on bottom half of wrapper. Put avocado slice and a few mint and basil leaves over lettuce. Using a slotted spoon, scoop 1/4 cup of noodle mixture onto lettuce.

Starting from the bottom, roll wrapper all the way over filling. Push back towards the bottom to tighten, and then fold sides over towards the center. Roll towards top. Place finished roll on a plate, and repeat with remaining wrappers, lettuce, avocado, herbs, and filling.

Cover and refrigerate rolls if not serving immediately. Just before serving, whisk dipping sauce ingredients together. Serve sauce in a small bowl next to rolls.

Seared Tuna with Avocado-Mango Salsa

Look for heavy, smooth-skinned, very fragrant mangoes that give a little under your thumb. With its vivid sunset colors and bright tropical flavors, this salsa also makes a fantastic topping for a bowl of black beans and rice.

1 ripe avocado, peeled, pitted, and cubed
1 large ripe drippy mango, peeled and chopped
handful of cilantro leaves, chopped
mild vegetable oil
juice of 2 limes
1/2 red onion, peeled and finely chopped
1 jalapeno pepper, seeded and finely chopped
salt to taste
2 hand-sized filets of tuna, mahi-mahi, or other meaty, steak-like fish, 6 to 8 oz each

Toss salsa ingredients together. Don't skimp on the lime and salt. If you're making it ahead of time, don't add the avocado and cilantro until just before serving.

Lightly oil up your grill. Get it good and hot. On the top of the stove, a grill-pan will need at least 5 full minutes to get hot enough. Brush fish filets lightly with oil. Sear for about 3 to 4 minutes per side, until outside is char-marked but inside is still juicy and cool.

Top with salsa and serve.

Bangkok Melon Salad

This irresistible sweet-salty salad was inspired by a dish once served at Ponzu, an Asian-fusion restaurant in San Francisco. On a winter day when there were no melons to be found, we made a surprisingly tasty variation using cubed papaya, sliced firm (green-yellow) bananas, and shredded Napa cabbage. Thai basil has narrow, purple-green leaves and a sharp anise scent that works better here than typical Italian-style basil.

1/4 cup water	1 fresh red chile pepper, minced
1/4 cup honey	1/2 cantaloupe, peeled and cubed
1 stalk lemongrass, finely chopped	1/2 honeydew melon, peeled and cubed
grated zest of 1 lime	1/2 a small watermelon, peeled and cubed
1/4 cup lemon juice	1/2 bunch cilantro, stems removed and leaves roughly chopped
1/4 cup lime juice	grated zest of 1 lemon
1/4 cup fish sauce	1/2 cup roasted peanuts, chopped
small thumb of fresh ginger, peeled and grated (about 1 tbsp grated)	1/2 bunch Thai basil leaves, stems removed and leaves roughly chopped

Combine water, sugar, ginger, lemongrass, and lime zest in a medium pot and bring to a simmer. Turn off heat and let steep for 10 minutes. Strain, discarding solids. Add juices, fish sauce, and chile and chill. Toss cubed melons with basil leaves and lemon zest. Add dressing to taste. Sprinkle with chopped peanuts just before serving.

Yam Balls

Much more than the sum of its parts.

2 large orange sweet potatoes, steamed or roasted, peeled, and mashed
1 cup panko (Japanese bread crumbs)
2 eggs, beaten
vegetable oil

Mix mashed sweet potatoes with 1/2 cup panko crumbs. Spread remaining panko on a plate. Pour beaten eggs into a shallow bowl. Form sweet potato mixture into balls, dip in beaten egg, and roll through panko crumbs. In a deep skillet over medium heat, heat 1" of oil until a small bit of potato mixture sizzles and sputters when dropped in. Slide as many balls into oil as will fit without crowding. Fry until golden brown, flipping over to brown the other side. Drain on paper towels and serve hot.

Pineapple Coconut Custards

During the baking process, hard, glossy caramelized sugar magically liquefies to become a delectable thin caramel sauce. Very easy and impressive... Substituting coconut milk for regular milk imbues this French-inspired dessert with the flavor of the tropics.

1/2 cup sugar	1 tsp rum
1/4 cup sugar	1 cup coconut milk
1 large egg yolk	1 tbsp butter
2 large whole eggs	rum to taste
1/2 fresh pineapple, peeled and sliced into flat triangles	

Preheat oven to 325°F.

Preheat oven to 325°F. Melt 1/2 cup sugar in a small, heavy saucepan over moderate heat. Swirl, don't stir, until it melts to the color of a dirty penny. Divide caramel among ramekins, tilting to thinly coat the bottoms (it's okay if bottoms are not completely covered). Be careful not to get it on your skin, as it's both very sticky and extremely hot. (Afterwards, fill the empty saucepan with warm water and let it soak. The hardened sugar will dissolve right off.)

Whisk together yolks, whole eggs, and a pinch of salt in a bowl. Bring coconut milk and remaining 1/4 cup sugar to a simmer. Pour hot milk into eggs in a slow stream, whisking constantly. Add rum.

Divide coconut mixture between ramekins. Put ramekins into a baking pan. Pour enough hot water into the baking pan to come halfway up the ramekins. Bake until set around edges with centers still jiggly, about 20 to 25 minutes. Using a spatula, transfer ramekins to a rack to cool. Once cool, transfer to the refrigerator to chill thoroughly before serving.

Just before serving, melt butter in a large skillet over medium heat. Add pineapple triangles and sauté until heated through and beginning to brown around the edges. Lower heat, add a splash of rum and cook another minute or two. To serve, run a knife around edge of each ramekin to loosen custard. Hold a plate tightly over ramekin and flip over, inverting custard onto plate. Top with several pineapple wedges.

Cancer

June 21-July 22

Symbol: Crab   Element: Water

Ruler: Moon   Quality: Cardinal

Swoon Me, Spoon Me

Ruled by that ol' devil moon, Cancers are swoony, spoony, moon-in-June-y romantics. They might hide under a hard shell, but inside, that crab's tender heart is yearning to be loved by a perfect one and only. Sweep a Cancer off his or her feet and you'll have a loyal and devoted lover for a long, long time. So where else to picnic but Paris, with a pique-nique fit for the Eiffel Tower?

Like their fellow water signs Scorpio and Pisces, Cancer body-surfs the ups and downs of emotional tides. Keep an eye on the calendar—full moons affect Cancers more than other signs. Emotions run high and their responses will be extra-intense. Women get all hormonal, men sensitive and maybe even a little weepy. And when times get tough, these crabs get tougher, retreating into their hard shells and hanging out the "Do Not Disturb" sign. And they're not above working a little superstition. Like when a Cancer pal was having a terrible time finding decent housing for herself, her girlfriend, and their sweetie-pie Pitbull-Rottweiler puppy. Her answer? Getting the dog's name tattooed on her forearm, inside a lucky horseshoe. It worked. And when she and her girlfriend got married, they tattooed on their wedding rings. See? This kind of love plays for keeps.

Still, the promise of a little slap and tickle—or more specifically, a good emotional heart-to-heart and an afternoon in bed with plenty of chocolate—can usually tease a Cancer from his or her shell. Get a Cancer out into the open air and sunshine, out of the pouty little cave in which they might like to hide… and bring a blanket, because these secret romantics adore an al fresco romp. On a beach, up against a tree, in the back of the car at the scenic overlook: Cancer has the admirable quality of turning anywhere into the best place for romance à deux.

One of the nice things about this menu is that you can cheat without anyone knowing. You may not be able to buy madeleines on the subway platform like on the Paris Metro (although you can find them in little 3-packs at Starbucks), but a baguette or two, a good bottle of wine, and some gussied-up pâtés make a very convincingly French spread without a lot of time spent in the kitchen. Keep that tender Cancer heart in mind, though, and don't dwell on what's in the pâté or rillettes over dinner. French charcuterie is very, very delicious, as long as your adorable little crab isn't getting all PETA-ish about the little bunnies and duckies that made it. If meat's not an option, look for vegetable terrines and tasty cheeses instead. Follow these with the first foods of summer—bright cherry tomatoes and crisp radishes dipped in coarse salt, a flaky-crusted quiche filled with melting, buttery leeks slow-sautéed to sweetness, and honey-drizzled strawberries trailed through thick, tangy Greek-style yogurt.

Besides the quiche and madeleines, this menu is more about shopping than cooking. Have fun at a good specialty shop or fancy deli sampling olives, cheeses, pâtés and terrines, and be sure to buy your French bread on the morning of your picnic, since it turns into a rock-hard baseball bat the day after.

With regards to le vin, rose is what you want. C'mon, it's pink! Everyone likes pink! I guess if you're wooing a really uptight straight guy or a particularly butch woman, you could replace the rose with a perfumey French white instead—like an Alsatian Riesling—or even a light red, like a Beaujolais or gentle Pinot Noir. (Heck, you can even bring beer! But not Bud. Try something tart and spritzy, like a Heffeweizen with a slice of lemon, please.) If you do decide to trust me and think pink, make sure you get an actual rose and not one of those next-door-to-a-wine-cooler white zinfandels, which are still lurking in some wine-store fridges, waiting to trap the unwary. If it's super cheap and says Sutter Home or "blush wine" on the label, it's not what you want. Thankfully, there are more and more good wines out there topped with picnic-perfect screw caps. Ditto for wine in a box, especially if you buy it at a place with bargain-gourmet pretensions, like Trader Joe's.

Menu

Paté, Rillettes, Terrine on Baguettes
Leek Quiche
Cheeses
Cherry Tomatoes, Olives, Radishes
Strawberries dipped in Greek Yogurt with Honey
Lemon Madeleines

Leek Quiche

You want to get lucky? Honey, make your own crust. It's NOT difficult, and there is NO comparison between even a half-assed homemade all-butter crust and one of those crappy cardboard-y store-bought frozen jobs. Trust me: Cancer will know the difference. If you use a food processor, it's pretty much foolproof. But you can also use your two hands, which are even more reliable, since they're easier to clean, for starters, and you always know where to find them. You can use sautéed spinach or chard instead of the leeks.

Crust:	Filling:
1 cup flour	2 tbsp butter
1/4 tsp salt	2 leeks, white and pale green parts chopped and rinsed thoroughly
6 tbsp butter, chilled	
2 to 3 tbsp ice water	pinch of nutmeg
	salt and pepper
	1 1/2 cups milk, half-and-half, or cream (or some combination thereof)
	3 eggs

In a large bowl, stir flour and salt together. Chop cold butter into small chunks. Using a pastry cutter (also called a pastry hoop), or the pads of your fingers, cut the butter into the flour. Flatten the bits of butter between your thumbs and fingertips, making flat, nickel-sized disks. Toss butter and flour lightly as you flatten. When butter has been reduced to oatmeal-sized flakes, start drizzling in ice water. Toss with a fork and add just enough water so that the dough will hold together in a ball when gently squeezed together.

Flatten into a round and wrap in plastic wrap (or pop into a resealable plastic bag). Chill in the refrigerator for at least 1 hour. (This makes the dough easier to handle and less likely to shrink and warp during baking.)

Lightly flour a large cutting board or countertop. Roll out dough into a round about 2 inches bigger than your pie plate. Roll from the middle outwards, lifting and turning crust every few rolls to keep it from sticking. (If you're worried about the dough sticking to your countertop, roll it out between two sheets of waxed paper. Or use a long offset spatula or butter knife to loosen dough from rolling surface.)

Fold dough in half, then in quarters. Move it to your pie plate, unfold, and gently fit into pan. Pinch the edges of the pastry into scallops or points. Wrap in plastic again and chill while you make the filling.

Preheat oven to 375°F. Melt butter in a heavy skillet over medium heat. Sauté leeks, stirring frequently, until softened and translucent. Season vigorously with nutmeg, salt, and pepper. Remove from heat.

In a medium bowl, beat eggs and milk together. Scoop in leeks. Pour mixture into crust and bake for 30-40 minutes, until crust is browned and center is firm, golden, and slightly puffed. Serve hot, warm, or room temperature.

Lemon Madeleines

Will these change your life, as they did Proust's? Who knows, but they're cute, cute, cute. For a brief, happy moment, a bunch of high-end French restaurants in New York City twigged to the universal appeal of these tasty little cakes. At the end of the meal, right before the check, they'd send out batches of warm, freshly-baked madeleines swathed in big white napkins—for free! Swanky and yet so sweet, they made me want to hand a big fat tip (and my phone number) to every waiter in the place. Yes, you'll need a special madeleine pan to get the proper scallop shape, but it's a small price to pay for turning your kitchen into your Cancer sweetie's favorite French bakery.

butter and flour for pan	1/2 tsp vanilla extract
2 eggs	1/2 cup flour
1/3 cup sugar	1 tsp grated lemon rind
1/4 tsp salt	4 tbsp (2 oz) butter, melted and cooled

Preheat oven to 375°F. Grease madeleine pan very thoroughly, getting into all the nooks and crannies. Shake flour over the pan, tilting and shaking to get an even coating over each cup. Turn the pan upside down and bang it firmly to remove any excess.

In a large bowl, beat eggs, sugar, and salt for at least 5 minutes, until the mixture has doubled in volume and looks thick, creamy, and pale, like a vanilla milkshake. (A hand-held electric mixer makes this easier, although a whisk and good biceps will work, too.) Beat in vanilla extract.

With a rubber spatula, fold in flour, followed by the lemon rind and melted butter. Spoon batter into prepared pan. Bake for 6 to 8 minutes for small molds, 10 to 12 minutes for larger ones, until tops spring back when touched and edges are golden brown.

Using oven mitts, flip pan over and bang against countertop to release madeleines. Use your fingers or a butter knife to pry out any that stick. Let cool on a rack. These are best served fresh out of the oven, although they'll stay fresh, well-wrapped, for 2 days.

Leo

July 23 - August 22

Symbol: Lion   Element: Fire

Ruler: Sun   Quality: Fixed

Fiery Roman Feast

Leo the lion needs no introduction. Ruled by the Sun, powerful Leo is the sign of high summer, when the sun is at its full strength at the zenith above the equator. As a fixed midsummer fire sign, Leos know their place… right there in the spot where everything (and everyone) revolves around them.

Like their namesake, Leos flourish when they're the kings and queens of the jungle, reigning happily from their throne at center stage. Luckily, they have more than enough talent to match their egos. No matter what the size of the audience, they're happy to provide a great show. Besides being natural leaders, fiery Leos know how to spark up a good time. Look for the storyteller at the center of any group, and chances are it's an August baby. With fire as their element, Leos thrive on conflagration. They like to be in the middle of any event, burning up the wires with brilliant ideas.

Love is central to these feisty lions, and they can be intensely passionate lovers, flaming hot while their emotions and intellects are engaged. Leo can also be in it just for the highs, though, and once the initial fire has burned out, they can be off in search of the next hot thing. A Leo in the early stages of romantic infatuation can be an impressive force of nature that's hard to resist, especially since their powerful natural charisma tends to create a magnetic swirl of crushes wherever they go. Enjoy the attention, but don't take their every grand proclamation of undying love as gospel, especially if you're a tender-hearted Pisces, Cancer, or Aquarius. Once they've spent a few years getting their fill of romantic drama, they'll be ready to make a solid commitment to their life-mate, and all those sweeps of grand passion will soften into real sincerity and true love. How many years constitutes "a few"? Only Leo knows.

Naturally, as summer sun worshippers, Leos love a barbecue. But where they'll want to be is right in the heat of things running the grill all night, getting greasy and smoky and bequeathing their juicy, charcoal-striped booty to the whole pride. I would bet you that a disproportionate number of barbecue pit masters—the ones who stay up, fueled by Pabst Blue Ribbon and pork rinds, to wet-mop their ribs and brisket for 16 or 18 hours at a stretch—are fire-loving Leos. So, throw a barbecue and put Leo at the center if you want some good, tasty carnivorish eating.

If you're looking to woo a Leo, however, don't do for them what they'd rather be doing for you. Instead, treat them like the fabulous Roman emperors they are, and bring the feast to them while they luxuriate in the attention (and the chance to lie back and be treated right). Spread out a grand banquet of Italian delights, starting with antipasti and ending with beautiful sweet peaches, a bowl of cool gelato, or a boozy, creamy pillow of tiramisu. First, they'll feast, and then they'll feast on you.

Menu

Antipasti
Pasta with Slow-Roasted Summer Tomato Sauce à la Susie
Shrimp Scampi
Insalata del Campo
Pepperonata with Zucchini
Tiramisu

Antipasti

These are lovely salty nibbly bits, made to tease and pique your appetite. If possible, find a good Italian grocery store, and choose a selection of olives, roasted red peppers, marinated artichoke hearts and other vegetables; sliced hard salami, soppressata, or proscuitto; thin breadsticks (grissini) or fresh crusty bread; and maybe some fresh mozzarella balls or a few cubes of Fontina cheese. Arrange on a platter and let Leo browse through while you garlic up the shrimp.

Slow Roasted Summer Tomato Sauce à la Susie

This recipe is adapted from the blog of Susie Bright. You may know Susie as an amazing writer, sex activist, and finger-on-the-pulse cultural critic. But she's also an incredible seamstress, cook, and Leo-loving Aries sensualista, and her recipe for this hot August tomato sauce is the most luscious thing ever. Don't be put off by the long cooking time—as Susie says, "While you're out fornicating or smashing the state, the tomatoes and peppers will be roasting like fallen angels." Serve over your favorite pasta.

2 lbs tomatoes, halved	1 tbsp balsamic vinegar
3 cloves garlic, peeled and chopped	1/2 tbsp honey
1 onion, peeled and quartered	1/2 tsp salt, or more to taste
2 sweet bell peppers, red, orange or yellow, seeded and halved	1 small bunch fresh basil
	3 tbsp olive oil

Preheat oven to 275°F. Drop tomatoes, peppers, garlic, and onion into a deep roasting pan (a 9" x 13" lasagna-type pan works fine, or any other large pan at least a couple of inches deep). Splash in olive oil, vinegar, honey, and salt. Squish around with your hands until all the vegetables are evenly coated.

Place the vegetables in your warm oven and let them slowly stew in their own juices for at least four or five hours.

Now, look in your cabinet. Do you have an immersion blender, a.k.a. a stick blender? If so, dump all your vegetables and their liquid into a saucepan. Shred up a handful of fresh basil and add it, along with a few fresh oregano leaves, should you have some. Using your immersion blender, buzz the veggies into a chunky sauce.

If not, shred a handful of basil and a few fresh oregano leaves over the vegetables in the roasting pan. Scoop vegetables and their liquid into a blender or food processor. (You'll probably need to do this in batches.) Pulse the veggies into a chunky sauce. Listen to Susie: "Now dip into the pan with your spoon and taste the results. You are not going to believe that you could have made something so divine, so deep, like a Sicilian oracle." Serve warm or room temperature tossed with your favorite pasta.

Shrimp Scampi

Shrimp, olive oil, lots of garlic: a foolproof combination. Cook the shrimp until just opaque,
as they can get rubbery if overcooked.

2 tbsp olive oil
3/4 lb large peeled raw shrimp
4 large garlic cloves, sliced
1/2 tsp dried hot red-pepper flakes
1/2 cup dry white wine
1 tsp salt
1/2 tsp black pepper
1/2 cup chopped fresh flat-leaf parsley
juice of 1 lemon

Heat oil in a heavy skillet over medium-high heat. Add garlic, red pepper flakes, wine, salt, and pepper to skillet and cook for a minute or so over medium heat, stirring, until garlic is just starting to turn a little golden. Add butter, stirring until melted, and then add shrimp. Stir for a minute or two, until shrimp is opaque but still silky. Sprinkle on parsley and lemon juice, and serve.

Pepperonata with Zucchini

Roasted red peppers are so smoky-sweet and delicious that you'll most likely find yourself slurping down half the peppers while you're still in the kitchen. So start with more peppers than you'll need. You can always feed them to your fire-loving Leo while you're cooking. The anchovy is optional, but adds a delectable, savory bass note.

3 red peppers (or more—see above)
3 cloves garlic, smashed and peeled
1 tsp anchovy paste (or a couple of salted anchovy fillets, well-rinsed)
2 tbsp olive oil

4 small young zucchini or other summer squash
2 tbsp flour seasoned with salt and a little red (cayenne) pepper
salt, freshly ground pepper
1 lemon

You need a grill, gas stove, or broiler for the first stage of this. If you're using a grill or broiler, grill or broil your whole peppers close to the heat, turning frequently, until skin has blackened all over and is beginning to blister and flake. If using a gas stove, turn up one burner to high. Using tongs or a long fork, turn the pepper around in the flame until the skin blackens and begins to blister and flake. Make sure all the skin turns black, since you're going to be peeling the little sucker later, and only blackened skin will peel off. Once your peppers are well charred, pop them into a bowl and cover. Let them steam in their own heat for 10 to 15 minutes.

Uncover and peel off all that blackened skin with your fingers. You may have to rinse the peppers briefly to get the charred specks off, but go easy, since you want to keep as much of those syrupy pepper juices as possible. They will be all limp and supple, with their sweetness all concentrated and smoky. Mmm. Cut into fat strips and set aside.

In a wide heavy skillet, heat olive oil, smashed garlic cloves, and anchovy. Nip the tops and bottoms off the zucchini, and cut into long slices lengthwise. Dust lightly with flour and fry in olive oil, turning once, until just tender and beginning to brown around the edges. Don't crowd the pan, as you want to sauté, not steam.

Lift zucchini out of the pan and arrange in a decorative way with the pepper strips. Sprinkle with a little salt, some more freshly ground pepper, and squeeze the juice of a lemon over the top. Add the olive oil, garlic, and anchovies from the pan if you want a funkier edge.

Insalata del Campo

At San Francisco's Delfina restaurant, this combo of salty pancetta, toasted walnuts, sweet-tart balsamic vinegar, and shards of Parmesan makes otherwise bitter greens completely irresistible. It's delightful at the restaurant, of course, but this is my kitchen-table approximation.

2 1/2 tbsp olive oil
1 tbsp balsamic vinegar
1 shallot, finely minced
salt and freshly ground pepper to taste
1/2 head radicchio
1/2 head frisee
handful of arugula
1/2 cup coarsely chopped toasted walnuts
4 thick slices pancetta or good bacon
parmesan wedge

Whisk together the oil, vinegar, shallot, salt and pepper. Core the radicchio and cut crosswise into thin ribbons. Tear the frisee into small pieces. Combine the radicchio, frisee and arugula in a salad bowl. Add the walnuts. Fry the pancetta or bacon slowly in a skillet until almost crisp. Drain briefly on paper towels, then cut into 1/4-inch-wide slices. Add to the salad.

Toss the greens with the vinaigrette. Taste and adjust seasoning. Using a vegetable peeler, shave as much Parmesan as you like into the salad. Toss again gently. Shave a little more Parmesan on top.

Tiramisu

When it comes to coffee, men wearing scarves, and dairy products, Italy wins. There's no American counterpart to real Italian mascarpone, which has the silky texture of sour cream and the taste of sweet butter. Search it out at Italian grocery stores or well-stocked specialty markets. And while you're there, look for Italian *savoiardi*: light, dry, spongy cookies that can soak up coffee and cream without falling apart.

2 cups very strong coffee, cooled	2-3 tbsp Marsala wine
1/3 cup sugar plus 1 tsp	10-12 ladyfingers or Italian *savoiardi*
1 1/4 cups mascarpone	1 tbsp unsweetened cocoa powder (not cocoa mix)
3 eggs	

Pour coffee into a large shallow bowl or deep plate to cool. Separate the eggs, discarding one white. In a large bowl, beat egg yolks with 1/3 cup sugar until thick, fluffy, and pale yellow, about 8 to 10 minutes. Add mascarpone and Marsala, beating thoroughly until smooth. Set aside. Beat egg whites until they form soft, droopy peaks when beater is lifted. Quickly beat in 1 tsp sugar. Using a rubber spatula or large spoon, fold the beaten egg whites into the mascarpone mixture.

Dipping first one side then the other, dunk each ladyfinger briefly into the cold coffee. Cookies should be well-moistened but not mushy. Closely line the bottom of a fairly deep dish with half the ladyfingers. Cover with a generous blanket of the mascarpone mixture. Using a small sifter, shake 1-2 teaspoons cocoa over the mascarpone. Top with another layer of coffee-soaked ladyfingers, arranged perpendicular to the first layer. Cover with the rest of the mascarpone mixture. Sift another 1-2 teaspoons of cocoa over the top.

Cover and chill for at least 4 to 6 hours, or overnight. Why? So the mascarpone mixture will firm up, the ladyfingers will soften, and all the flavors will commingle into a big cuddle party of Italianate goodness.

Rise and Shine

Morning is Virgo time, and they've got places to go, people to see, a puggle to walk, and a Pilates class to teach. Serve up a healthy, tasty brunch with just enough effort to make it fancy without fuss, and Virgo will be heartily appreciative. Prompt, punctual, and detail-oriented, Virgos do have a rep as the copy editors of the zodiac, dotting i's, crossing t's, and stemming pop culture's ever-rising tide of sloppy half-assedness. But far from being uptight, being demons of organization means Virgos can be incredibly productive, so they can save the world, throw a party, find a home for a pair of stray puppies, repaint the kitchen, go salsa dancing, and sing Dolly Parton karaoke... all in one weekend.

You desire a devil-may-care type who'll sprint off to a gas-station restroom in bare feet? We'll bet our Jimmy Choos you're not going to find her in this part of the zodiac. She won't even have a Virgo rising, or be on a Virgo cusp. But (again) this doesn't mean Virgos are always uptight. In fact, they're often ever-curious travelers on a lifelong quest for information and knowledge about the world. And if they turn down a date by claiming they're off to scale Machu Picchu or check out Antarctica's penguins next week, believe them. They'll have the passport stamps (and Flickr postings) to prove it when they get back.

What they'll put up with on the road and how they live at home are two different things, however. Vacuum up the cat hair and Swiffer the kitchen floor before you invite Virgo over. Spit and polish is the Virgo way, and they'll have a hard time relaxing in a grubby environment. A Virgo knows where her comb is at all times, and both her house and her fine self are well-groomed, good-looking and welcoming, even first thing in the morning. If you need mouthwash, she can close her eyes and tell you exactly on which shelf in the medicine cabinet you can find it. They're brushed and glossed and pedicured at all times, with beautiful sparkly eyes that draw admirers from across the room, and if this sounds fussy, I've got two words for you: Sophia. Loren. A Virgo through and through. Likewise Sean Connery, Raquel Welch, and Chrissie Hynde (a tough rocker chick—but have you ever seen her without eyeliner?).

Despite their diva-ish reputation, Virgos—like soufflés— aren't really that tricky to master. Their only unwavering demand is that they be served the minute they're ready. Any hanging around, and they'll collapse gracefully into a tasty but unimpressive heap. Tell a Virgo to be at your door at 11 a.m., and you can count on him or her to be punctual to the minute—an admirable trait, and one absolutely worth rewarding with a tower of fluff.

Did you know that Virgos get along famously with other Virgos? Just as Libras bask in the glow of their fellow Libras, the beauty and organization of some Virgos can only be truly appreciated by another Virgo. So if you're a September baby, enjoy the smarts (and clean kitchen!) of your fellow Virgo, and toast your good fortune with a (properly opened) bottle of bubbly. Everyone else, well, mop the floor, match your earrings to your panties, iron the napkins, and enjoy that sweet Virgo charm.

Menu

Cheese Soufflé
Berry Muffins
Fruit Platter
Chicken Apple Sausage or Meatless Sausage Patties
Sweet Potato Hash or Green Salad

Cheese Soufflé

This recipe is adapted from an equally foolproof one in Fran Gage's wonderful cookbook, *Bread and Chocolate: My Food Life in and Around San Francisco*. Remember, once you've poured your fluffy mixture into the soufflé dish, leave the kitchen and go chat up your fascinating Virgo vixen. Absolutely no peeking allowed for at least 25 minutes! (Use the oven light and squint through the smeary little window if you must, but don't open the door. An even temp is crucial for achieving maximum fluff.) When done, it should be dramatically puffed and golden brown, with a center that's a bit jiggly but not soupy. Take out of the oven and serve at once.

4 tbsp (1/2 stick) butter
4 tbsp all purpose flour
1 1/4 cups whole milk, warmed
1/2 cup white wine
4 large eggs, separated
1 tsp salt

freshly ground black or white pepper
4 oz fresh goat cheese, crumbled, or the same amount of cheddar or Gruyere, coarsely grated
1 tbsp grated parmesan cheese, optional
2 tbsp finely chopped chives

Position rack in center of oven and preheat to 400°F. Generously butter a straight-sided ceramic soufflé dish. Separate the eggs, putting the whites in a large bowl. In a small bowl, beat the yolks lightly with the salt and pepper.

In a heavy saucepan over medium-low heat, melt butter. Add flour. Stirring constantly, cook without browning for 2 minutes. Whisk in warmed milk. Whisking constantly, cook until smooth, thick and bubbling, about 2-3 minutes. Add wine and cook for 1 to 2 minutes. Remove from heat. Add egg yolks and whisk quickly to blend.
Stir in cheeses and chives, and set aside.

Using an electric mixer or a clean whisk, beat whites in large bowl until they form glossy peaks when beaters are lifted. Using a rubber spatula, fold 1/4 of whites into lukewarm soufflé base to lighten. Using a gentle up-and-over motion, fold in remaining whites, turning bowl as you go. Stop when whites seem mixed in about 3/4 of the way. Scoop into prepared soufflé dish. Bake soufflé until puffed, golden and gently set in center, about 30 to 35 minutes.
Serve immediately.

Berry Muffins

These sunny, wholesome muffins will make your whole kitchen smell oh so sweet and buttery. Bake them before you put the soufflé in the oven, so you'll have something to nosh on with your mimosas and coffee while the soufflé bakes. Frozen fruit works just fine in these, too. No thawing necessary; just throw in the berries straight from the freezer.

1 cup all-purpose flour or whole wheat pastry flour
1 cup cornmeal
2 tsp baking powder
1/2 tsp baking soda
1/2 tsp salt
3 tbsp sugar or honey, or more to taste
2 eggs

1 cup buttermilk, or 3/4 cup plain or vanilla yogurt beaten with 1/2 cup milk
3 tbsp melted butter or mild vegetable oil, such as canola or safflower
1 cup blueberries, raspberries, or blackberries
1/2 cup chopped pecans
optional: 1/2 tsp cinnamon mixed with 2 tbsp sugar

Preheat oven to 350°F. Lightly grease a 12-cup muffin pan, or line with those cute little paper baking cups. In a large bowl, sift or stir together flour, cornmeal, baking powder, baking soda, salt, and sugar.

In a separate bowl, beat together honey (if using instead of sugar), eggs, and buttermilk. Pour wet mixture into dry. Using a wooden spoon, stir ingredients together until just mixed. Do not beat!
Pour in melted butter, berries, and pecans, and mix gently.

Spoon into prepared muffin pan. Sprinkle with cinnamon sugar if desired. Bake 20-25 minutes, until muffins are just golden and firm to the touch. Place on a rack to cool for 5 minutes, then remove muffins from pan, running a butter knife around the edges of each cup to loosen, if necessary. Serve warm with butter and jam.

Fruit Salad

Bigger is better when you're making fruit salad. Weensy dice looks chintzy, while nice big chunks look lavish. Use a thematic blend of three or four kinds of fruit so the flavors stay distinct. Got a melon baller? Your Virgo guest will be the one to appreciate it. Otherwise, cut your fruit into even chunks or slices. Bananas may seem like an obvious choice, but they're better left out, since they quickly turn slimy. Strawberries, too, fade and go squishy if added too far in advance.

A splash of fresh lemon, lime, or orange juice will keep the cut fruit from browning. A swirl of honey boosts sweetness, and a judicious glug of almond or orange-flavored liqueur always adds a certain appealing je ne sais quoi. Real Amaretto de Serrano is gorgeous, but even cheapo Amaretto is usually all right. For anything orange-flavored, though, go for a classy liqueur like Grand Marnier or Cointreau. Low-rent orange booze will make the whole thing taste like powdery little baby aspirins… not the effect you're aiming for here.

Some suggested combinations:

honeydew and cantaloupe balls
blackberries
chopped fresh mint
juice of 1 lime

sliced white and yellow peaches
or nectarines
raspberries
juice of 1 lemon
1 to 2 tbsp amaretto

sliced plums
pitted sweet cherries
blueberries
1 tbsp honey and/or 1 tbsp Chambord (berry liqueur)

fresh pineapple chunks
mango cubes
papaya cubes
green grapes, halved
juice of 1 lime
sprinkle of fresh coconut

sliced oranges and tangerines
sliced Asian or Anjou pears
pomegranate seeds
1 to 2 tbsp Grand Marnier or Cointreau

Sweet Potato Hash

Why sweet potatoes? Well, any diner can turn out halfway decent home fries. This chunky orange hash looks better, tastes more interesting, and gives a snappy color contrast to the pale-golden soufflé. And sweet potatoes are packed with vitamins, always a plus for health-conscious Virgos. Leftover cooked sweet potatoes can be used. Not canned, though—they're too squashy.

2 sweet potatoes, scrubbed and cubed

1 tbsp oil

1/2 tsp paprika

1/4 tsp oregano

1/2 tsp chile powder

1/4 tsp salt, or to taste

Pile sweet potato cubes in a vegetable steamer and steam until just barely tender. Heat up oil in a heavy skillet over medium heat. When oil is good and hot, add sweet potato cubes, sprinkling on herbs, spices, and salt. Let sauté for 5 minutes, then shove around with a spatula. Continue to cook, flipping cubes around (but not mashing them) until browned around the edges and cooked all the way through. Serve hot.

Libra

Sept 23 - Oct 22

Symbol: The Scales

Ruler: Venus

Element: Air

Quality: Cardinal

Mezze at the Oasis

Hello, party people! Like Taurus, Venus-ruled, extravagantly sensual Libra is a master of the pursuit (and creation) of pleasure. As an Air sign, though, dainty Libras will only get their hands dirty behind the scenes. However, while the earth-bound Taurus glories in excess, the Libran appetite is fueled by curiosity and a sense of adventure. They love to taste and nibble a wide array of alluring foods, and will happily eat off your plate if you've got something intriguing there. In the most delightful way, of course—as the party people of the zodiac, Librans care about their manners. (That 1954 edition of Emily Post on the bookshelf? Mid-century kitsch, of course, but count on your Libran pal to have read it cover to cover at least once.) And while they won't turn down a luscious chocolate truffle or a handful of French fries, their innate sense of balance keeps their diet in check. If it's rich or indulgent, they'll enjoy it—but a bite or two will be enough to satisfy.

Being the first sign of fall, whose reign begins just after the autumn equinox, Libras are naturally drawn to the colors and tastes of the harvest season. Those blazing maples and glowing pumpkins? Just Mother Nature playing tribute to her favorite child, in the Libra's humble opinion. Like their fellow Cardinal signs Aries, Cancer, and Capricorn, Libras love beginnings best. The challenge is to keep the Libra palate alert and amused. Tie the social Libra down to a rigid procession of plates, and charm and appetite will wilt before dessert. Instead, keep the meal aloft through a delectable array of appetizers, with a meal that bounces lightly through a revolving series of fresh starts.

Able to see any question from all sides, Libras often find making a decision—even about where to go to dinner, or what to order once they get there—to be an agonizing exercise in limitation. Thai sounds good, but so does Indian; the duck breast sounds fabulous, but look, the pork chop comes with corn pudding! Being a restaurant critic is actually a dream job for Libra; they'll use their wit and charm to avoid hurting anyone's feelings, and they'll rejoice in an excuse to taste what's on everyone's plate.

Save the down-and-dirty funk—the stinky cheeses, the menudo and marrow bones—for dark, earthy souls like Sagittarius and Scorpio. Librans have a taste for sweetness and perfume, whether it's a honeyed Muscat or a cooling scatter of cilantro and mint. Libras also hate to stop talking, especially at a party, so make your snacks bite-sized and easy to munch, with an emphasis on beautifully colored of fresh fruits and vegetables. Bring on the roses and orchids, the sparkle confetti, flattering lighting, silky pillows and a chaise lounge or two. . . Libra likes to drape and lounge and dazzle with those sexy legs.

Again, like Taurus, Libras love attention, especially when it comes attached to a task at which they can shine. A plate of cookies to pass, a platter of strawberries to share, even some dishes to wash if it's the sort of party where everyone's hanging out in the kitchen—Libras like to be circulating through the center of the action, especially if they can show off a cute apron in the process. And they won't let less-than-perfect equipment get in the way of impressing their sweetheart.

I still remember the French toast made for me in my college boyfriend's dorm room. As a Libra cooking for another Libra, he knew elegant indulgence was the way to go. So he soaked fresh challah into a bowl of beaten eggs—adding milk was for wimps—then fried it in lots of butter in an against-the-rules electric frying pan. Then he added piles of raspberries, real maple syrup, more butter, and a mug of hot coffee with cream. Oh, and did I mention he was 18 at the time? Just one of the many reasons why we're still friends, and why his wife is a very lucky woman. Like Virgos, Libras adore their own kind, and there's no more successful party-throwing machine than a multi-headed hydra of Libras.

How to charm these social butterflies? By throwing them a party, where they only have to do the fun things—licking baklava-sticky fingers, popping grapes into willing mouths— instead of, say, running out to three stores to find bamboo skewers at the last minute. Invite Libra as the guest of honor, ply her (or him) with something sparkly and strawberried to drink, and sneak kisses in the pantry whenever you can. Brazen heavy petting in full view of all the guests isn't the Libra style, but a little naughtiness out of sight can work just fine. Compliments work, too: Libras bask happily in the glow of snappy banter and flirtatious approval.

And once the other guests go home, then it's time to whisk the dishes out of sight and draw a candlelit, rose-petal bath for two... with the leftover grapes and strawberries and sweets (hey, who left these chocolate truffles here?) next to the tub.

Menu

Hummus with Pita
Carrot Mint Salad
Lamb-Ginger-Cilantro Meatballs (Kefte) with Yogurt Dip
Raw Vegetable Crudites
Mozzarella-Tomato-Olive Skewers
Grapes, Melon, Strawberries
Baklava

Hummus

Sure, you can buy little plastic tubs of hummus in any supermarket. But this is the real stuff: lemony, garlicky, just right for scooping up with warm pita bread. Leftovers make a super sandwich filling, stuffed in a pita with sliced tomatoes and Carrot Mint Salad.

1 can (15 oz) chickpeas, drained
1 clove garlic, or more to taste
1 tsp salt
1/3 cup water
1/3 cup tahini (sesame paste)
1 tbsp olive oil
juice of two lemons

Put garlic clove on a cutting board. Using a small flat-bottomed drinking glass, smack clove until skin pops off. Peel off skin and discard.

Put garlic, chickpeas, salt, and water in the blender or food processor. Blend for 1 minute. Turn off blender and scrape down the sides with rubber spatula. Replace the lid and blend again for another minute, or until mixture is smooth. Add tahini, olive oil, and lemon juice and blend for another minute. Taste for seasoning, and add more lemon juice or salt as needed. It will get more garlicky-tasting as it stands, so go easy.

Using rubber spatula, scrape hummus into a bowl and drizzle with olive oil. If not serving immediately, cover the bowl with plastic wrap and refrigerate. Serve with warmed pita triangles.

Carrot Mint Salad

Bright, wholesome, and pretty, and the mint adds a slightly exotic Moroccan touch.
Very nice with hummus in a pita sandwich.

1 lb carrots, organic if possible, peeled and coarsely grated
1/4 cup olive oil
2 to 3 tbsp lemon juice
a splash of apple cider vinegar
salt and pepper
a large handful of fresh mint leaves, stems removed, finely chopped

Toss carrots with olive oil, lemon juice, vinegar, salt and pepper. Taste and adjust seasonings as necessary.
Just before serving, stir in mint.

Lamb Kefte Kabobs

The exact proportions of cilantro, scallions, parsley, and ginger aren't really important here; it's the combination of flavors that sparks up the lamb. You can also make these in burger-sized patties, served on toasted buns with chutney or a spicy ketchup.

1 lb ground lamb

1/3 cup finely chopped cilantro (a generous handful, stems removed)

1/2 tsp salt

1 thumb-sized knob of ginger, peeled and grated

2 scallions (green onions), chopped finely

1/3 cup finely chopped parsley (a generous handful, stems removed)

Preheat broiler and line broiler pan with aluminum foil. Using your clean hands, gently mix lamb with herbs, grated ginger, scallions, and salt. Form into small balls. Slide onto metal skewers, two or three per skewer. Broil 5 minutes or so on each side, or until outside is well browned but centers are still pink. Remove from skewers and serve with toothpicks and yogurt dip.

Yogurt Dip

Inspired by Greek tzatziki and Indian raita, this makes a cooling dip for the hot lamb meatballs. Look for unwaxed cucumbers, or peel it completely if it's waxed. If your cuke is watery and seedy inside, scrape out the seeds with a teaspoon before grating.

1 cup thick Greek-style yogurt

1 small cucumber, grated

a generous handful of mint or dill, stems removed, finely chopped

1 scallion (green onion) or 1/2 small red onion, finely chopped

salt and pepper to taste

Stir yogurt, cucumber, mint or dill, scallions, and salt and pepper together. Taste for seasoning. If not using right away, cover and chill.

Baklava

Delicate pastries soaked in flavored honey syrups are a traditional specialty of many Middle Eastern cuisines. But the Greek baklava, with its irresistible layers of rich nuts and crackling-thin golden pastry, is perhaps the best known, with good reason. Look for frozen phyllo dough in the freezer section next to the pie shells and puff pastry. Let it defrost overnight in the refrigerator, as frozen phyllo is brittle and more apt to crumple and crumble. While assembling your baklava, always keep a damp cloth over the bulk of the sheets to keep them from drying out.
A pastry brush will help immensely with the buttering.

2 cups walnuts, blanched almonds, or pistachios, or a mixture of all three, finely chopped

2 tbsp sugar
2 tbsp honey
pinch of salt

1/2 lb phyllo, defrosted
1/2 cup butter, melted

One of the following flavorings: 1 tsp grated orange and 1/2 tsp ground cardamom;
1 tsp cinnamon and a pinch of ground cloves; 1 tsp rosewater; 1 tsp orange flower water

Honey syrup:

1/3 cup sugar   1/2 tbsp lemon juice
1/2 cup honey   1/3 cup water

One of the following flavorings: 1/2 tbsp grated orange rind; 1 stick cinnamon or
1/4 tsp ground cinnamon; 1/2 tsp rosewater

Preheat oven to 325°F. Lightly grease an 8" x 8" baking pan. Unfold phyllo dough and trim into 8" x 8" squares. Cover sheets with a damp cloth. In a small bowl, mix finely chopped nuts, sugar, honey, salt, and your choice of flavorings. Spread a phyllo sheet over the bottom of the baking pan. Using a pastry brush, lightly brush sheet with melted butter.

Baklava (cont.)

Repeat with 5 more sheets, lightly buttering each sheet before adding the next. Spread approximately 2/3 cup of nut mixture over 6th phyllo sheet. Layer 4 sheets (buttering each one) on top of the nuts. Spread another 2/3 cup of the nut mixture on top sheet, and top with another 4 sheets (buttering between each one). Spread with last 2/3 cup of nut mixture. Top with 6 sheets, buttering each one and finishing with a final layer of butter.

Using a sharp knife, make four equal vertical cuts (about 1 ½ inches apart) through the top layer of pastry. Then make eight equal diagonal cuts (approximately 1 inch apart) across these strips to form 18 diamond shapes. Bake for 30 to 35 minutes, until pastry is crisp and pale golden.

While baklava is baking, make the syrup. In a heavy-bottomed pan, heat sugar, honey, lemon juice, and water to boiling. Keep a close eye on it, as the syrup will froth and foam up. Add orange rind, cinnamon stick, or ground cinnamon, if using. Over medium-low heat, simmer for 10 minutes, until syrup has thickened slightly.
If using rose water, add now.
Remove from heat and pour into a pitcher. Let cool.

Pour syrup over hot pastry. (Alternately, let pastry cool to room temperature before cutting. Reheat syrup to almost boiling, then pour hot syrup over cool pastry.) You may not need all of the syrup. Following the previously made cuts, cut pastry all the way through into diamonds and let syrup soak in for at least 3 hours before serving.

Note: The trick to ensuring a crunchy, sticky pastry is to pour cool syrup over hot pastry, or hot syrup over cool pastry. As long as the pastry and syrup are opposite in temperature when they come together, you won't end up with soggy baklava.

Scorpio

Oct 24 - Nov 22

Symbol: Scorpion Element: Water

  Ruler: Pluto   Quality: Fixed

Midnight Feast of Love

Deep and dark, baby, that's what you get with Scorpio. While its symbol is the scorpion, protecting its desert home with a barbed and poisonous sting, the astrological Scorpio is a water sign with a shortcut to the subconscious. Of all the signs of the zodiac, roiling, stormy Scorp is the most receptive to mysteries and unseen psychic forces. Empathetic, secretive, and emotional, they are also under the sway of Pluto, whose slow transit through the zodiac is marked by generational periods of upheaval and drastic change. Pluto is, of course, named after the Roman counterpart to Hades, the Greek ruler of the underworld.

In other words, Scorpios are heavy, man. Before the identification of Pluto in 1930, Scorpio was tied to Mars, which might explain Scorpio's reputation as a sensual powerhouse with a jealous streak and a taste for trouble. (And given the astronomers' recent demotion of Pluto from planet back to asteroid, Scorpio may well get its Mars ruling back for good.) Eros and Thanatos—that is, sex and death, and their attendant impulses towards creation and self-destruction—are the ruling forces in the world of Scorp. Give Scorpios a bunch of roses, and they'll get a kick out of the thorns as much as the petals.

In the Western hemisphere, late-autumn Scorpio is also connected with the waning of the harvest, the time when, according to Greek mythology, the pomegranate-munching Persephone returned to Hades, leaving her mother, the harvest goddess Demeter, to mourn her loss in wintry chill. But as a fixed sign, Scorpio is also connected with preservation, stubbornness, and endurance. The undertow of their water element pulls them down below the surface into the dark depths of both body and soul. Romance with a Scorp is a meaty affair. Dragged (willingly) into the Scorpio cave, you might just have the best sex of your life, if you don't melt from the heat of your demon lover.

All this to say, don't count on making it out of the house for that dinner reservation. When Scorpio comes over, it's best to have the pantry well stocked with lustful edibles. Plan a meal that can be eaten in stages, with a chance in between to work up your appetite again. Only rich and earthy flavors assuage the Scorpio's hungers. Think aged port and blue cheese, blood-red beets and plump figs dipped in sticky, tart-sweet pomegranate syrup. And, of course, chocolate: dark and molten in a seething volcano of hot raspberries and gooey cake batter.

This is a menu suitable for one of those massive goes-to-eleven Cabernets, the kind led snarling from a cage. There's no wine too potent, no tannins too mountainous for deep, dark Scorpio. On a budget? Look for Hungarian Bull's Blood, also known as Bikavér, a spicy, concentrated wine with firm tannins and peppery-berry flavors. Cheap but effective, just like red lipstick, black satin, and fishnet stockings… all surefire Scorpio-pleasers.

Menu

Tamasin's Chicken Livers
Figs & Pigs
Lamb Chops with Port Sauce
Ruby Beet Salad
Bleeding Heart Cake

Tamasin's Chicken Livers

The pungency of freshly crushed spices turns these earthy livers into hot and delectable little nubbins. If you don't have a mortar and pestle, try using a small metal bowl and a heavy-bottomed mug or sturdy glass. Why Tamasin? Because the idea for these came from *Good Tempered Food*, an extremely alluring cookbook by Tamasin Day-Lewis, sister of Daniel and a star in the Brit food world.

1/2 lb chicken livers (from the happiest, most humanely-raised chickens you know), cleaned and de-veined
1 tsp whole cumin seeds
1/2 tsp coriander seeds
1/2 tsp coarse salt (coarse sea salt, fleur de sel, or Malden salt)
1/2 tsp whole black peppercorns
1 tbsp flour
pinch of cayenne
1 tbsp butter plus a splash of olive oil

Rinse and pat livers dry. Toast the cumin and coriander in a dry pan over low heat for 30 to 40 seconds, until they smell fragrant and just ever so slightly toasted. Pour into a mortar (or metal bowl), add salt and peppercorns, and grind or crush together until cracked and chunky. Stir in flour and a pinch of cayenne.

Pour spice mixture onto a place and roll the livers around in it. Heat up the butter and olive oil in a skillet. Let it get good and hot, then tip in the livers. Let them sizzle and spatter for a couple of minutes, then flip them over to the other side to cook for another minute or two.

Slice into one liver to check for doneness—you want them still pink and soft inside.
Scoop onto a plate and serve while still spitting-hot.

Figs & Pigs

Want to get your heart's desire from a Scorpio? Sit on his or her lap and feed him or her these lush little morsels one by one. (Have I done this? You bet.) Savory and salty-sweet, they get their moan-inducing quality from pomegranate molasses, a Middle Eastern condiment made from fresh pomegranate juice boiled down into a tart, intensely fruity syrup.

1/3 cup pomegranate molasses

2 tbsp balsamic vinegar

10 to 12 fresh figs

4 oz proscuitto, in sheer, drapey slices

4 oz crumbled blue cheese or mild goat cheese

Preheat oven to 425°F. In a small saucepan, combine pomegranate molasses and vinegar. Over medium heat, bring to a simmer and let cook, stirring frequently, until mixture has reduced by half and become syrupy. Remove from heat and set aside.

Using a small sharp knife, cut an X through the top of each fig. Stuff in a small piece of cheese. Slice the proscuitto lengthwise into wide strips. Wrap a strip of proscuitto around each stuffed fig. Place on a baking sheet and drizzle lightly with the pomegranate syrup. Bake for 3-5 minutes, until proscuitto is just beginning to crisp and figs are plump and oozy. Drizzle with any additional syrup. Pick up a warm, sticky fig and feed to your sweetie. Repeat.

Lamb Chops with Port Sauce

Like most of the other elements in this meal, you can pick up these meaty little chops and eat them with your fingers, swishing them through the sauce on your way.

4 lamb loin chops

Marinade:	Sauce:
1/2 cup red wine	2 tsp butter
1 tbsp red wine vinegar	3 tbsp minced shallot (1 to 2 shallots)
1 tbsp minced shallot	1/2 tsp flour
2 cloves garlic, peeled and crushed	1/3 cup port
2 tbsp olive oil	1/3 cup dry red wine
generous pinch of salt	1 tsp balsamic vinegar
	salt and freshly ground pepper
	generous pinch of thyme

Whisk together marinade ingredients and pour into a bowl big enough to fit the lamb chops in a single layer. Add chops and let marinate for 1 hour.

Preheat the broiler. In a small, heavy saucepan over medium-low heat, melt butter and sauté shallots, stirring frequently, until softened and clear, 2 to 3 minutes. Add 1/2 tsp flour and cook, stirring, for 1 minute. Add port and red wine, and let simmer for 2 to 3 minutes. Add balsamic vinegar, salt, pepper, and thyme. Cook for another minute or two, until mixture thickens slightly and looks syrupy. Taste for seasoning and remove from heat.

Broil chops for 2 to 3 minutes. Turn over and broil for another 3 minutes. This should give you nicely pink chops; reduce or increase the timing depending on how rare or well-done you like your chop. Drizzle with sauce and serve.

Ruby Beet Salad

Making beet lovers out of beet haters, such is my mission in life, and this salad is my never-fail secret weapon. The tart, almost winy flavor of the pomegranate molasses elevates beets to ecstatic new heights.

1 bunch beets (3 or 4 beets)
2 oranges, preferably blood oranges
2 tbsp pomegranate molasses, or more to taste
1/4 cup olive oil
salt and freshly ground pepper

Preheat oven to 350°F. Rinse beets and place them, still wet, on a square of aluminum foil. Fold the foil around them to make a nice little package. Pop in the oven and roast until you can slip a knife easily through both beets. If there's any resistance, let them roast some more; the more tender, the better. Remove beets from oven and let cool in packet. When beets are cool enough to handle, slip off skins. Cut into wedges and set aside.

Grate the zest from one of the oranges and toss with beets. Cut zested orange in half and squeeze in the juice. Drizzle on pomegranate molasses, olive oil, and salt and pepper to taste. Toss and taste for seasoning. Cover and refrigerate for at least 1 hour. Just before serving, peel and slice remaining orange, and add to salad.

Bleeding Heart Cake

A gush of raspberries at the center of a deep, dense, molten chocolate cake...if any dessert could convince a Scorpio to howl at the moon when you're gone, this is it. Splurge on the dark chocolate you most adore. This recipe was inspired by the signature molten-chocolate cake of my friend Chad, who's as nice and straight-up a guy as you'd ever want to meet. But I'm convinced he has a dark side, if only because of his love for this very wicked cake.

1/2 pint fresh raspberries	2 oz good-quality dark chocolate, chopped
1 tbsp sugar	3 tbsp unsalted butter
1 tbsp Chambord or crème de cassis (optional)	1 large egg yolk
butter for greasing ramekins	1 large egg
2 tbsp unsweetened cocoa powder	2 tbsp all purpose flour
1/4 cup powdered sugar	powdered sugar for serving

Toss raspberries with 1 tablespoon sugar, and liqueur, if using. Set aside.

Preheat oven to 350°F. Butter two ramekins, Pyrex dishes, or custard cups. In a small bowl, stir together cocoa and 1/4 cup sugar. In a small heavy saucepan over low heat, melt chocolate and butter together, stirring frequently until both are melted and mixture is smooth. Remove from heat and whisk in cocoa mixture. Whisk in egg yolks, then whole egg. Sprinkle in flour and stir gently to blend. Half fill ramekins with batter. Drop a spoonful of berries into the center of each ramekin, then cover with remaining batter.

Preheat oven to 350°F. Bake cakes uncovered until edges are set but center is still shiny. A toothpick inserted into the center should come out still gooey, about 20-22 minutes.

Run a butter knife around edges of each cake to loosen; unmold onto plates.
Sift a little powdered sugar over each cake and surround with remaining raspberries.

Sagittarius

Nov 23 - Dec 21

Symbol: Archer

Element: Fire

Ruler: Jupiter

Quality: Mutable

Shot Through the Heart

Half-person, half-horse, straddling the end of autumn and the beginning of winter, Sagittarius is a intriguing bundle of contradictions. First and foremost, they are travelers in body and mind, spurred on by curiosity, restlessness, and a longing for adventure and discovery. Prodigious in both energy and intellect, they're full of opinions and ideas, ready to work round the clock to put their dreams into action.

Highly intellectual, they're also passionately physical, and at their best, can be irresistible scholar-athletes, or just really smart swoon machines. Find a charming rock-climbing geek who's also a great kisser, and chances are he or she's a Sag. Start-ups are made for Sagittarius, since along with their problem-solving abilities and long-range visions, they're also the zodiac's great optimists, with enough independence and natural recklessness to make them willing to take the risks necessary to get a wild idea off the ground. They're also excellent at being their own bosses, since their blunt, tell-it-like-it-is style can make them seem a little abrasive. But that's the Sag way: if you want to get to the truth, you shoot an arrow straight towards the target. Like Gemini and Virgo, Sag is a seeker.

As you can already guess, Jupiter, the big guy, is their ruling planet, giving them an extra-hefty dose of luck, optimism, and wanderlust. These are not homebodies but explorers, always willing to trade the tried and true for the next new thing, which can extend to their relationships as well. Great flirts as they are, this doesn't necessarily mean they're getting it on with a different honey every night; instead, it can mean that they like to keep even the home fires burning hot, whether this means bringing intriguing new toys into the bedroom or throwing you on the back of their brand-new motorcycle for a spin around town.

As a fire sign, they can be quick to ignite in anger. Once they blow up, though, it's over, and they're ready to laugh at themselves and move on. Delicate sensibilities need not apply; Sag needs a work-hard, play-hard partner to ride along, especially one with well-developed interests and a fulfilling career. Like Aries, Sag loves a chase, and you'll match up well if you can keep up a flirtation that combines intellectual challenges with some fiery booty action, coupled with a mutual need for independence.

Sag also likes to win. Remember Harry Potter's centaurs, who freaked out at the notion of being ordered about (or worse, ridden) by humans? That's Sag for you. In other words, it's all fun and games until you get in the saddle and start hauling in the reins. So, fight, fight hard, then let them win (or better yet, do your own thing, and let them keep up with you).

When it comes to the table (and the bedroom), Sag loves to experiment. Hey, what can happen? That's their mantra, which can mean four-star triumph, or fleeing the premises for a burger down the street. (And speaking of adventure, Sag supposedly has a thing for both hot talk and back-door action. Can't speak from experience on this one, but so I've been told. Just saying.) Whether you're cooking or chasing, don't be timid with a Sag in your sights.

Save the tried-and-true—the mac n' cheese, the reliable roast chicken, the Victoria's Secret lace teddy—for comfort-food types. Instead, splash out with a theme. Whether it's a Burmese feast, a Gothic menu all in black, or just hot peppers and a blindfold, Sag will roll with whatever you come up with so long as it's done with brio. In this case, think of the archer ready to shoot for his supper. (Just like Ted Nugent, that bow-hunting, NRA-supporting, libertarian rock'n'roller: is it any surprise that The Nuge is a Sag born smack in the middle of December?)

For this dinner, imagine your Sag has dragged home a wild boar, and it's up to you to use it in as many delicious ways as you can. The result? Sweet and salty pig candy to start, followed by tender pork chops with hot-pink braised red cabbage, and the pièce de résistance, a lard-crusted, open-faced pear galette. If you're pig-phobic, you can substitute a stuffed dumpling squash for the chops, and butter or shortening for the lard. As for the appetizer, candying turkey bacon might work. If you're going totally vegetarian, skip those leathery fakin'-bacon strips for rounds of soy "Canadian bacon," and bake until just crunchy but not dried out.

Menu

Pig Candy

Pork Chops with Apples and Quince

Stuffed Winter Squash

Braised Red Cabbage

White Salad

Winter Pear Galette

Pig Candy

Nope, it's not candy for pigs, it's candy from pigs!

8 slices (about 1/2 pound) bacon
1/4 cup firmly packed dark brown sugar
1/4 tsp or more cayenne pepper, or some other tasty chile pepper powder—try ancho, chipotle, even smoked paprika

Preheat oven to 350°F. Rub bacon with sugar and pepper. Line a baking sheet with parchment paper or foil and place a wire rack on top of the sheet. Arrange the bacon in a single layer.

Bake until bacon is crisp and browned, about 20 minutes, rotating the sheet pan in the oven to make sure it browns evenly. Remove from rack and blot on paper towels before serving.

Pork Chops with Apples & Quince

Sure, you can make this with just apples. But quinces add a spicy, savory note that gives the pork an extra dimension of late-fall yum. Quinces look like fuzzy, deep golden, lumpy apples with a rich fragrance. They are rock-hard and astringent when raw, but turn tender and deep blush pink when cooked.
Use a heavy, very sharp knife to hack into slices.

2 tbsp butter
2 inch-thick pork chops
1 flavorful, firm apple, like Braeburn, Cortland, or Macoun, cored and sliced
1 quince, cored and sliced

1/2 cup apple cider
generous splash of half-and-half or heavy cream
1 branch fresh sage
salt and freshly ground pepper

In a large, heavy skillet over medium-high heat, melt 1 tbsp of butter. Rub chops with salt and pepper, then brown for 2 minutes per side. Transfer to a plate. Add quince slices and 1/4 cup apple cider, and cook, turning frequently, until softened. Add apple slices and cook, turning frequently, until golden. Lift out fruit and add to plate with chops.

Pour the rest of cider into the pan. Let it cook down for several minutes, scraping up any browned-on bits from the pan with a spatula. Return chops and fruit to the pan, and add a splash of half-and-half or heavy cream along with the sage. Cover and cook over medium heat for 15-20 minutes, until chops are cooked through and sauce has reduced a bit. Remove chops and fruit to a platter. If necessary, simmer sauce for a couple of minutes, until thickened. Taste for seasoning, pour sauce over chops and serve.

Stuffed Winter Squash

You (or your sweetie) not down with the pig? Use this tasty stuffed winter squash as your entrée instead. Come Thanksgiving, these are also a festive way to fill the turkey-shaped hole on vegetarians' plates. Sweet dumpling squash (a relative of the delicata that looks like an indented, oversize cupcake) is the perfect size and shape for stuffing. As for the rice, you can use one cup of those tasty mixed-rice blends you find in the bulk bins at the health food store, in lieu of the brown and wild rice.

2 sweet dumpling or other meaty fist-sized winter squash
3/4 cup brown rice
1/4 cup wild rice
1/2 tsp salt
2 tbsp butter or olive oil
1 large yellow onion, peeled and chopped
2 carrots, peeled and chopped

1 stalk celery, chopped
2 cloves garlic, peeled and chopped
1/2 cup chopped mushrooms (white button, cremini, or portobello)
2 or 3 leaves fresh sage, minced
2 branches fresh thyme, or 1/4 tsp dried thyme
salt and freshly ground pepper
1/2 cup pine nuts or chopped pecans, lightly toasted
1/2 cup dried cranberries or apricots

Preheat oven to 350°F. Cut off the tops of the squash and scoop out the seeds and strings. Pour 1/2 cup of water into a baking pan and add squash, cut side down. Bake for 35 to 45 minutes, or until the inside is moist and tender.

In a small, heavy pot with a tightly fitting lid, cover brown rice and wild rice with 1 3/4 cups water and 1/2 tsp salt. Bring to a boil, reduce heat to very low, and cover. Let simmer for 40 minutes. Turn off heat and let steam for another 15 minutes.

Meanwhile, heat the butter or olive oil in a large skillet. Sauté chopped onion, celery, and carrot until onion is translucent and carrot and celery are just tender. Add garlic, mushrooms, and herbs, and sauté until mushrooms are tender. Add rice to contents of skillet, tossing well. Add nuts and cranberries, and taste for seasoning.

Mound rice stuffing into your squash. If necessary, pop into a 350° F oven for 10 minutes to reheat.

Braised Red Cabbage

A sweet-sour, hot-pink accompaniment to the pork or squash. This keeps well, and can be made a day in advance.

1 tbsp oil

1/2 head red cabbage, thinly sliced

1 small yellow onion, peeled, halved, and thinly sliced

1/4 tsp salt (or to taste)

2 tbsp red wine or apple cider

1 to 2 tbsp red wine vinegar

2 tsp brown sugar

a generous pinch or two of thyme

freshly ground pepper

In a deep skillet, heat oil over medium heat. Add onion and sauté, stirring frequently, until softened and translucent. Add cabbage and salt and cook, stirring frequently, until cabbage begins to go limp. Add wine or cider and sauté until nearly evaporated. Add vinegar, sugar, thyme, and pepper. Cook, stirring every few minutes, until cabbage is as tender as you like, 10 to 15 minutes more. For very soft cabbage, add a little water and cover the pan while sautéing. Taste and adjust vinegar, sugar, and salt to taste.

White Salad

A cool all-white salad for winter, sparked up with jeweled beads of fresh pomegranate and wedges of fresh orange.
Be sure to remove all the bits of bitter white pith when you're digging out the pomegranate seeds,
and watch out for (or embrace) crimson juice splashes!

1 head Belgian endive
1 handful frisee
2 small turnips
1 daikon radish
1 pomegranate, peeled, seeds removed
1 navel or blood orange, peeled and sliced

Dressing:
1 tbsp white wine or champagne vinegar
1 tsp Dijon mustard
3-4 tbsp olive oil
salt and pepper to taste

Slice endive into narrow strips. Toss with frisee. Peel turnips and radish and cut into thin slices. Add to endive and frisee. Whisk dressing ingredients together and taste for seasoning. Toss endive mixture with dressing.
Top with orange slices and pomegranate seeds.

Winter Pear Galette

Lard, lard, gift from the pig-loving gods to all pastry-makers. I don't mean the additive-laced stuff in cardboard boxes found over by the margarine in some supermarkets. If you have access to a good butcher shop or a farmers' market selling humanely raised pork, ask around for rendered leaf lard, made from the fat around the kidneys. It has a waxy texture and a rich, meaty smell, and will make the flakiest, most flavorful pie crust you can possibly imagine. It will keep almost indefinitely in the freezer.

Crust:	Filling:
2 cups flour	2 lb pears, cored and sliced
1/2 tsp salt	juice of 1 lemon
1 tsp sugar	1/2 cup brown sugar, packed
6 tbsp fresh rendered leaf lard, frozen	1/4 tsp powdered cloves
6 tbsp (3/4 stick) butter, chilled	1 tsp flour
	1 tsp minced candied ginger, or 1/4 tsp powdered ginger

Egg wash, for shininess: 1 egg beaten with 2 tsp water

granulated sugar, for sprinkling

In a large bowl, stir flour, salt, and sugar together. Chop cold lard and butter into small chunks. Using a pastry cutter (also called a pastry hoop), or the pads of your fingertips, cut the butter into the flour. Flatten the bits of butter between your thumbs and fingertips, making flat, nickel-sized disks. Scoop up and toss the flour lightly as you flatten. When fat has been reduced to oatmeal-sized flakes, start drizzling in ice water. Toss with a fork and add just enough water so that the dough will hold together in a ball when gently squeezed together.

Winter Pear Galette (cont.)

Flatten into a round and wrap in plastic wrap (or put into a plastic bag). Chill in the refrigerator for at least 1 hour.
(This makes the dough easier to handle and less likely to shrink and warp during baking.
But if you're in a rush, you can skip right to the next step.)

Lightly flour a large cutting board or countertop. Roll out dough into a nice big, even round. Roll from the middle outwards, lifting and turning crust every few rolls to keep it from sticking, using a spatula or butter knife to loosen dough from rolling surface. (If dough seems particularly sticky or annoying,
roll it out between two sheets of waxed paper.)

Fold dough in half, then in quarters. Move it to a lightly greased baking sheet. If it's a hot day in your kitchen, drape the baking sheet lightly with plastic wrap and pop it back in the fridge. Meanwhile, core and peel your pears, then slice into eighths. Toss with lemon juice, sugar, flour, and spices. (Again, if time is of the essence, and you're fine with a more rustic look, it's perfectly fine to skip the peeling.)

Preheat oven to 400°F.

Take out your baking sheet, and arrange pears on the dough in concentric circles from the outside in, leaving a 3-to-4-inch wide bare margin along the outer edge. Once you've filled in the rest (and you can double-layer here and there if you need to, since the pears will shrink while cooking), fold the surrounding pastry crust over the edges, pleating as you go. Brush with egg wash, sprinkle with a little sugar, and bake for 35 to 40 minutes,
until crust is golden brown and fruit is tender. Remove from oven, and cool on a rack for 1 hour.
Serve warm or room temperature; best eaten the day it's made.

Capricorn

Dec 22 - Jan 19

Symbol: Goat

Element: Earth

Ruler: Saturn

Quality: Cardinal

Down to the Marrow

It's true: Capricorns can be a little touchy. But just look at the calendar: can you blame them? These cute little goats never got to bring birthday cupcakes into school because all the kids were out on winter break. Their birthdays got steamrolled by Christmas, Chanukah, or New Year's. By the time their big day rolled around, everyone in the family was too wiped out, hung over, or maxed out to hire a pony or bake a big sparkly cake. So Capricorns learned to be stoic and pretend "Like, hey, no big deal, I'm self-reliant, I don't need anyone to make a fuss over me. I'll just get my take-out coffee and my free meal at Denny's and it's cool."

Of course, this is a big lie. Capricorns long to be made much of. But they prefer one-on-one activities to a big splash. Pay attention to what they like. Like their fellow earth signs Taurus and Virgo, they are creatures of habit at home, and they do love their sensual pleasures. At the same time, their cardinal aspect makes them go-getters who set high goals, shoulder multiple responsibilities, and work hard to make life better for others. But they also appreciate getting their needs met, even if they won't admit it at first.

Like Saturn, their ringed ruling planet, they have many scenes and activities orbiting around them, so it may take some effort to unhook them from their tangle of post-work obligations and meetings. It's worth it, though: Capricorns are devoted and loyal, and once you've got their attention, they'll put their hard-charging passion to work on you. And like their symbol—the goat—they also have a playful, curious side. Tease them, make them laugh, and they can surprise you with their willingness to unknot their ties or kick off their pumps and loosen up.

Once they're finally giggling, ply them with good food and wine, and see what they'll spill as those rocky defenses come down. These are not your make-out-on-the-dance-floor, play-hooky-for-nooky types; what you'll get once Capricorn makes a commitment is a stable, hard-working, upright and dedicated partner. Which, after you've run around with one too many flaky hotties, can start looking pretty darn good. It's not that they don't have deep feelings; after all, they're ruled by Saturn... planet of secrets, mysteries and seismic change. They just don't reveal them easily, and for all their clarity of communication in the workplace, they can have a hard time finding words to define the workings of their hearts. Don't push them. They'll come across eventually.

Intimacy, once it's been earned, is an aphrodisiac for the goat: you'll probably have your best times in the sack after a heart-to-heart chat that turns confessional. And again, take your time. Capricorns prefer the slow burn, and control hounds that they are, they like to feel like they're the ones taking the initiative. And remember: work usually comes first, which means fooling around on a school night is a special treat, not a given. Hold out for the weekend, and make sure to get your action written into Cap's busy schedule.

Oh, and watch out for that temper. Let's just say Capricorns know how to get into touch with their anger. Luckily, they also known how to use humor to defuse sticky situations, and if they're not taking themselves too seriously, they'll often joke themselves right out of a blow up.

So, what to serve? As the first sign of winter, Capricorns have an affinity for the deep, dark foods of December and January: sturdy roots and tubers, cold-hardy greens, dried fruits, nuts, ale, whole grains, and winter herbs like bay laurel, rosemary, and juniper. Meat works, as do aged cheeses, and savory, salty dishes. Their palates seek satisfaction rather than titillation, and they can have high standards when it comes to judging food and wine, although their down-to-earth tastes lead them more towards well-executed basics rather than gourmet frou-frou. Luckily, you can't go wrong with a rich, slow-cooked beef stew, redolent with red wine and herbs, served over a nutty farro pilaf and followed by a mineral-rich beet and spinach salad dotted with toasted walnuts and goat cheese. Pair this meal with a big, fleshy red wine—an earthy French burgundy, perhaps, or a California zinfandel full of plums and pepper. With the Black Tart, pour a glass of Port, or a good, slightly smoky single malt Scotch.

Menu

Chestnut Soup
Beef Stew with Red Wine
Seitan with Red Wine & Chestnuts
Farro Pilaf with Dried Mushrooms
Spinach Salad with Roasted Beets, Goat Cheese & Toasted Walnuts
Black Tart

Chestnut Soup

Inspired by the smooth-as-velvet bisque served in wintertime at Café Sabarsky, an elegant Viennese cafe inside Manhattan's Neue Gallerie, this easy soup tastes much richer and more luxurious than its simple ingredients would imply.

12 to 15 fresh whole chestnuts,
or 12-15 peeled whole vacuum-packed or jarred chestnuts
2 tbsp butter
1 onion, peeled and diced
2 cloves garlic, minced
2 carrots, peeled and diced
1 parsnip, peeled and diced
1 branch thyme
4 or 5 sprigs of parsley, minced
1/2 cup dry sherry or Madeira
3 cups chicken broth
2 tbsp crème fraiche or sour cream

To prepare whole chestnuts, cut an X in the skin of each chestnut with a sharp knife. Roast at 325°F until the meat is tender and the skin dries out and curls back. Peel chestnuts while still hot, otherwise skin will stick to the nut.

Melt butter in a saucepan. Sauté onion, garlic, carrot, and parsnip, stirring, until tender. Add crumbled chestnuts and sherry, and cook, stirring, over low heat for 2 or 3 minutes. Add herbs and chicken broth, a little salt (depending on the saltiness of the broth) and simmer gently for 35 to 40 minutes. Let cool for a few minutes, then puree in a blender. Taste for seasoning, adding more sherry as needed. Return to the pan and warm gently.

Top each bowl with a spoonful of crème fraiche or sour cream.

Beef Stew with Red Wine

Your classic French-inspired beef stew. Warming, hearty, and even better a day (or two) after it's made, so you can put it together one day and serve it the next. This makes more than the two of you will need for one meal, but again, who doesn't love them some tasty French leftovers for lunch? If you make your beef stock, that's swell. Otherwise, use a low-salt brand with as little nasty junk (like MSG) in it as you can find.

1 tbsp olive oil	2 cups beef or chicken stock
4 oz bacon, sliced and then cut into squares	1 tbsp tomato paste
2 lbs beef chuck, cut into 2-inch chunks	1 tsp dried thyme, or several branches of fresh thyme
2 onions, sliced	1 bay leaf, fresh if possible
3 carrots, peeled and cut into chunks	12 small pearl onions, peeled
2 cloves garlic, minced	10 oz mushrooms, stems nipped off
2 cups red wine	2 tbsp butter
	approx. 1 cup water or chicken stock

Preheat the oven to 250°F. In a large, heavy Dutch oven with a cover, sauté the bacon in the oil for about 10 minutes, until lightly browned. Remove bacon and reserve. Toss beef cubes with salt and freshly ground pepper. Add beef to oil and bacon grease in pan and sauté until browned. You may have to do this in two batches—each batch should take 2 to 3 minutes. Remove beef and reserve.

Add sliced onions and carrots to oil in pan and sauté for 10 minutes. The onions will absorb the fat and get limp, golden-brown, and glistening—a beautiful sight. Add garlic and sauté for another minute. Add red wine, beef broth, and tomato paste, bring to a simmer, and cook down for a few minutes. Add beef, bacon, thyme, bay leaf, and a generous sprinkle of salt and pepper. Bring to a gentle simmer, cover, and put in the oven for two to three hours, until meat is tender enough to separate into moist shreds when pressed with a fork.

Beef Stew with Red Wine (cont.)

While stew is cooking, cook pearl onions and mushrooms. Heat a good tablespoon or so of butter in a wide sauté pan over medium-high heat and lay the mushroom slices down in one layer only (you may have do this in batches, depending on the size of your pan). Jostle the slices around so they all get nice and buttery, and then leave them alone. Let them get well and truly brown on the first side before you flip them over. When well-browned, remove from heat and set aside.

Place onions in a single layer in a smallish pot. Add a tablespoon of butter and enough chicken stock or water to barely cover. If using water, salt it well. Over low heat, simmer the onions in their nice buttery-salty bath, stirring frequently, until the liquid is reduced to a few syrupy tablespoons and the onions are very tender. Keep a sharp eye on them as the liquid gets low; onions are quite high in natural sugars and will scorch very easily. Mix with mushrooms and set aside.

After two hours, check stew and taste for seasoning. Is the beef really, really tender? Okay then, take it out the oven. (If not, replace the lid and let it keep cooking. Although it may seem tempting, raising the oven temp will NOT help. The only thing that will break down that chewy connective tissue is time and slow, moist heat, and sometimes it just takes a while.) Add cooked onions and mushrooms and simmer on top of the stove, uncovered, for five or ten minutes, until sauce has thickened slightly. Taste for seasoning. If cooking ahead of time, transfer stew to a bowl, let cool to room temperature, then cover and chill until needed.

Seitan with Red Wine & Chestnuts

A rich, winy stew, a little like a vegan beef bourguignon. The seitan cubes take on a deep ruby-red color, and the chestnuts add a sweet protein complement. Authentically (if quirkily) Italian, since I first had it at a tiny *agriturismo* in Sardinia, where it was part of a vegetarian feast made for us by Magdalena,
the farm's Roman-born, vegan-minded owner.

2-3 tbsp olive oil
1 onion, diced
1 carrot, diced
1 celery stalk, diced
300 gms (10 oz) seitan, cubed
2 cups red wine
1 bouquet garni of 2 parsley sprigs, 1 sage sprig, 2 thyme sprigs, and a bay leaf, tied together with string
1/2 tsp salt, or to taste
1 cup whole cooked, peeled chestnuts

In a deep, wide sauté pan or Dutch oven, warm olive oil over medium heat. Add onion, carrot, and celery, and sauté while stirring 10 minutes, until very soft but not browned. Add seitan cubes, red wine, salt, and bouquet garni. Bring to a simmer, reduce heat, cover, and simmer for 20 minutes. Add chestnuts and simmer covered for an additional 30 minutes. Uncover and simmer for 5-10 minutes, until flavors are blended and sauce has thickened a bit.
Taste for seasoning. Serve over Farro Pilaf.

Farro Pilaf with Dried Mushrooms

Farro? What's that? So glad you asked! It's a cousin to spelt, a precursor to wheat. A whole grain (tasting a little like brown rice, buckwheat, or barley), look for farro in Italian groceries or specialty food stores. Short-grain brown rice or kasha can be substituted if you can't find farro.

2 tbsp olive oil
1 small onion, diced
4 fresh sage leaves, chopped
1 sprig thyme
big pinch of salt
1 1/3 cups farro
2-3 cups vegetable, beef, or mushroom broth, warmed
1/2 oz (or to taste) dried porcini mushrooms, rinsed lightly and cut into smallish pieces
freshly ground pepper

Sauté onion, sage, and salt in olive oil for 3-4 minutes, until just translucent. Add farro, stirring to coat the grains thoroughly. Add one cup broth, cover, and let simmer over low heat. Check and stir frequently. When all broth has been absorbed, add next cup, and porcini bits. Keep checking—when all broth has been absorbed, taste and see if it's still chewy. If so, add a little more broth and cook a bit longer. It should be slightly chewier than rice.
You can stop just before it's done, turn off heat, and let it steam under cover for 5 minutes or so.
Add freshly ground pepper and taste for salt.

Spinach Salad with Roasted Beets, Goat Cheese & Toasted Walnuts

Roasting beets is a mess-free way of cooking these magenta-dripping babies. Thanks to the indirect heat, it's hard to overcook them (in fact, it's better to err on the side of cooking them more rather than less, so you get that tender, almost jellylike texture). And once they're cooked and cooled, the skins slip right off—a good trick to know, since peeling raw beets is a complete finger-staining pain. To toast the walnuts, spread them in a cake pan and bake at 300°F for 10-15 minutes, until lightly browned and toasty smelling.

a bunch of fresh spinach, washed thoroughly and dried, any thick stems removed

2 beets, tails trimmed and tops removed (save tops to cook like greens on another night)

3 oz fresh goat cheese (chevre), crumbled

1/2 cup walnuts, toasted

Dressing:
1 tbsp balsamic vinegar
1 tsp Dijon mustard
1 clove garlic, crushed but left whole
3-4 tbsp olive oil
salt and freshly ground pepper to taste

Preheat oven to 350°F. Rinse beets and place them, still wet, on a square of aluminum foil. Fold the foil around them to make a nice little package. Pop in the oven and roast until you can slip a knife easily through both beets. If there's any resistance, let them roast some more; the more tender, the better. Remove beets from oven and let cool in packet. When beets are cool enough to handle, slip off skins. Cut into wedges and set aside.

Whisk dressing ingredients together, and taste for seasoning. Just before serving, toss spinach with half the dressing, adding more as needed. Stir remaining dressing into beet wedges. Top spinach with beet wedges, crumbled cheese, and toasted walnuts. Serve.

Black Tart

Thanks to the prunes, raisins, and red wine, the filling of this tart really is black, which is cool by itself. But even better is how it perfumes the house with a deep medieval scent of winter at bay—a whiff of whiskey, a breath of ginger and cinnamon, a sparkle of fresh tangerine. The dried fruits aren't poached as much as steeped. After a slow warming, they sit on the back of the stove for an hour or so, swelling soft and plump as they absorb the wine and spices.

Sweet tart dough:
2 1/2 cups all-purpose flour
1/4 cup sugar
1/2 tsp salt
12 tbsp (1 1/2 sticks, or 6 oz) butter, chilled
2 egg yolks, lightly beaten
1 tsp vanilla extract
1 tbsp water, or more as needed
1/2 cup heavy cream, whipped, for serving

Filling:
1 large apple, peeled and diced
1 cup each dried apricots and prunes, diced
1/2 cup raisins
2-3 tbsp candied orange peel
1 cup red wine
1/4 cup whiskey
1/8 tsp each cinnamon and ginger
big pinch of freshly ground pepper
1/2 cup each brown sugar and white sugar,
or to taste (you can substitute 1/3 cup honey for the white sugar)
zest and juice of 1 tangerine
1/2 cup toasted walnuts, chopped

Make the dough: In a large bowl or the bowl of a food processor, mix or pulse together the flour, sugar, and salt. Chop the butter into 1-inch chunks. If mixing by hand, rub flour and butter chunks between your thumbs and fingertips to make flat nickel-sized flakes. Toss the flakes to coat with flour, then continue rubbing until it looks like dry oatmeal flakes. Drizzle in egg yolks, vanilla, and water. Toss lightly with a fork until dough can be lightly squeezed together into a ball, adding a few more drips of water if absolutely necessary. If using a food processor, drop in butter chunks and pulse until butter forms pea-sized clumps. Drizzle in egg yolks, vanilla, and water, and pulse briefly until dough just comes together.

Press gently into a flat round, wrap in wax paper or pop into a resealable plastic bag. Refrigerate for at least 1 hour or overnight.

Make the filling: In a heavy-bottomed pot, mix all filling ingredients except for the walnuts. Warm over low heat for 15 minutes. Turn off heat, cover, and let fruit absorb the rest of the liquid for an hour or so. Add chopped walnuts.

Divide the tart dough into two rounds and roll out. Line a 9-inch tart pan (the metal kind with crinkly edges and a removable bottom works best, but you can use a regular pie pan in a pinch) with one round of dough. Spoon in filling.

Cut remaining dough into narrow strips. Lay strips in a crisscross pattern to cover most of the filling. Chill in the fridge for an hour or so.

About 10 minutes before you want to bake the tart, preheat the oven to 375°F. Bake until crust in golden brown and filling is bubbling, about 35 minutes. Cool and serve with whipped cream.

The Chicken or the Egg?

Think of the never-ending stream of stars pouring from the celestial Aquarius's water jug, and you'll start to clue in to the Aquarius vibe. Bright ideas—some brilliant, some goofy—are continually bubbling up in the lively Aquarius brain. Ruled by far-reaching Uranus, they're the hitchhikers of the galaxy, ready to go snorkeling in Bali or llama-trekking in Peru. They'll try anything once. And if anyone's going to get off the plane with a phone number, it's going to be Aquarius, naturally curious and unself-conscious. They're much too interested in the world beyond them to care about their sense of cool—which, of course, just makes them that much more cool for being so unpretentious.

Aquarius makes friends easily and has a black book of couches on which to crash from Seattle to Katmandu. They're not players, though—their hearts are too tender, and their sensibilities too loyal for that. Instead, they're great matchmakers, setting up pairings from within their wide and remarkably diverse circles of friends and acquaintances. For themselves, Aquarius is often willing to jump right in if the chemistry is right, trusting that a serious commitment will follow just as easily.

A goofy sense of humor and a footloose love of travel are musts for Aquarius's partner, since with Aquarius behind the wheel, you never know where you might end up, and silly jokes can go far in keeping a road trip fun when it's 11 p.m. on a holiday weekend and all the motels for 3 states are booked solid. (Yes, this did happen to me and an Aquarius sweetie. What did we do? Finally found a bed in room 12A—as in 13—of an exceedingly scruffy highway motel, only to be woken at 4:30 a.m. by the revving pickup trucks of all the deer hunters staying next door. So we got up, found a rest stop with a Starbucks, and won $10 on a New York State lottery machine, which made it all better. Oh, and we made up a song about it, to the tune of "Good Night, Irene," to sing throughout the rest of the trip.)

Even as they'll willingly scarf down barbecued guinea pig out on the road, many Aquarians, like others whose signs are fixed firmly in the middle of their season, find it very restful to come back to the same old thing. If it works, why mess around? It's this fixed quality that keeps such an airy sign from floating off into the clouds. After all, impressing you with their globe-trotting culinary acumen is what they'll do when they invite you over. When they're at your house, give them the all-American comforts of home.

This Southern-inspired dinner is so old-fashioned that it's new again—after all, when was the last time you had cheese grits and pickled peaches? If you don't have the oven space to navigate the grits and the roast chicken at the same time, you can substitute a good-quality rotisserie chicken from your favorite market or takeout place, or make a batch of cornbread earlier in the day. Do make the devilled eggs, though—they are a snap to make and never fail to be both impressive and adorable.

Menu

Devilled Eggs
Roast Chicken
Southern Cheese Grits
Pickled Peaches
Buttered Peas
Hummingbird Cake

Devilled Eggs

As easy as pie—actually, much easier. You can flavor the eggs with anything—curry powder, wasabi, pickle relish, whatever. Just don't use too much, since you don't want to overwhelm the taste of the eggs. Sprinkle a little paprika over each egg before you serve them. Try using Spanish smoked paprika (*pimenton*) for a change if you happen to have some lying around the house.

3 or 4 eggs

2 tbsp mayonnaise

1/2 tsp prepared mustard

generous pinches of salt and pepper to taste

1/4 tsp of curry powder

OR 1/2 tsp pickle relish OR 1 tsp chopped fresh herbs (tarragon, dill, chives, parsley) OR 1/4 tsp prepared wasabi, optional

plain or smoked paprika for garnish

Put eggs in a saucepan and cover with cold water. Bring to a gentle simmer, then turn down heat and simmer for 10 minutes. Take pot off heat. Fill pot with cold water. Let eggs stand in cool water for 15 minutes. Peel eggs and slice each one in half lengthwise. Scoop out egg yolks into a small bowl. Mash egg yolk with mayonnaise, mustard, salt and pepper, and the flavoring of your choice to form a creamy paste. Taste for seasoning, adding more mayonnaise if mixture looks dry. Divide filling between egg-white halves. Sprinkle with paprika.
Serve immediately, or drape loosely with plastic wrap and chill until serving time.

Roast Chicken

Get a good, all-natural chicken, and baste when you think of it. Roast chicken is super-easy and it's always a hit. I used to drive myself crazy making all kinds of fancy things for friends when they came over for dinner, until I had this epiphany: roast chicken and cake! And now I'm much more relaxed, and everyone cleans their plates.

1 nice chicken, on the small side (about 2 1/2 to 3 lbs)
1 tbsp butter
1 lemon, halved
2 cloves garlic, roughly chopped
salt, pepper, paprika

Preheat oven to 350°F. Rinse and pat dry your chicken, remembering to pull out the little bag of entrails stuck inside. Run your fingers along the edge of the chicken skin around the cavity, loosening the little pockets above the legs. Slip the chopped garlic under the skin. Rub on the butter. Squeeze on lemon and put lemon halves into cavity. Rub with salt and pepper, and sprinkle on paprika. Put into a roasted pan, using one of those nifty V-shaped roasting racks if you have one.

Let roast for about 20 minutes per pound, basting every 30 minutes or so. It's done when the skin is crisp and browned and the legs wiggle freely. Insert a small, sharp knife in the thigh. The juices should run clear and the meat should look firm and opaque, not pale and slippery.

Remove from the oven, tent with foil, and let rest for 5-10 minutes before serving. Meanwhile, scrape up all the grease and tasty juices in the pan—we'll call this the jus, just to be all French and classy. Pour into a glass measuring cup, or if you're smart, one of those nifty grease-separating pitchers with the spout at the bottom, so you can get to the good stuff without disturbing the layer of fat on top. Let juices settle, then pour off and discard excess clear grease. Serve jus in a small pitcher or gravy boat alongside the chicken.

Southern Cheese Grits

Having a thing for Southerners means sweet-talking over a plate of cheese grits. Real Southern-style cheese grits should have so much grease in them that they fry themselves right in the pan. Even if you don't go quite that far, they still taste mighty good.

Sourcing good stone-ground, freshly milled grits can be a challenge if you don't live in the South. You can substitute coarsely ground polenta, although it's not the same thing. If all you can find are supermarket grits, be sure to go for the "old-fashioned" version, not the instant. If you're truly dedicated to your grits (and trust me, a displaced Southerner will kiss your feet if you hand them a plate of almost-like-their-mama's cheese grits) you can order them from Matt and Ted Lee, two displaced Southerners turned NYC hipsters who now run the Lee Bros. Boiled Peanuts Catalog, a mail-order company selling grits, country ham, hot pepper jelly, Cheerwine, and more.

1 cup stone-ground coarse grits
5 cups water

Bring water to a boil. Stir in grits, lower the heat to medium-low and cook, stirring frequently, until thick and porridge-y, about 25 minutes. They will spit and spatter like molten lava, so be careful. Mix in:

4 cloves garlic, peeled and minced
2 tbsp butter
8 oz cheese, grated*

2 eggs, beaten
1/2 tsp paprika or smoked paprika
(start with a 1/4 tsp of smoked, and add to taste)
Salt, pepper, Worcestershire sauce and Tabasco to taste

Preheat oven to 400°F. Sauté garlic in butter over low heat until just softened but not browned. Mix grits together with garlic (and any butter left in the pan), cheese, eggs, and paprika, along with just enough salt, pepper, Worcestershire sauce, and Tabasco to give it a little pep. Pour into a baking dish and bake for an hour, or until a nice golden crust is formed.

*Jaime from Tulsa will swear this needs to made with Velveeta. Kristen from Florida made a killer version in my kitchen using a big chunk of Irish cheddar. Being a Yankee, I'd probably vote for the Cheddar, but suit your own taste.

Pickled Peaches

A little bit sweet, a little bit tart—make these the night before so the peaches have time to soak up the spices. Whole spices keep the syrup clear; before you substitute ground cinnamon and cloves, look in the back of the cabinet for that fancy tin of 'mulling spices' that you used once to make hot spiced wine last Christmas. If peaches are out of season, you can use frozen peach slices or, in a pinch, canned. Not the ones in heavy syrup, though—look for the healthier ones, canned in juice.

1/2 cup apple cider vinegar
1/2 cup water
2 cinnamon sticks, broken in two
10 whole cloves
10 whole allspice berries
2 lbs ripe peaches

Bring a large pot of water to a rolling boil. Drop peaches in boiling water for one minute. Scoop out with a slotted spoon and let cool in colander.

While peaches are cooling, combine sugar, vinegar, water, and spices in medium saucepan. Add 1/2 cup water; bring to a boil. Stir until sugar dissolves, reduce heat and simmer 10 minutes.

When peaches are cool enough to handle, slip off skins with a paring knife. (If using frozen or canned peaches, begin here.) Cut peaches into medium-thick slices. Pour hot spiced syrup over peaches and let cool to room temperature. Cover and refrigerate overnight.

Hummingbird Cake

Another Southern classic, this sweet vanilla cake is bursting with chopped pecans, pineapple, banana, and orange rind. Looks like a carrot cake from the outside, thanks to the cream-cheese frosting, but tastes lighter and fruitier.

2 cups flour
1 tsp baking soda
1/2 tsp salt
1 cup sugar
2 large eggs, beaten
1/2 cup vegetable oil
1 tsp vanilla extract
1 cup chopped pecans
2 cups chopped bananas
1 tsp grated orange rind
1 (8-oz) can crushed pineapple in juice, undrained

Frosting:
4 oz cream cheese
4 tbsp softened butter
1/2 cup powdered sugar, or to taste
1/2 tsp vanilla extract
1/2 cup chopped pecans

Preheat oven to 350°F. Lightly grease and flour a 8" x 8" square pan. Whisk or sift together flour, sugar, baking powder and salt. Stir in eggs, oil, vanilla, pineapple (including juice), 1 cup pecans, bananas, and orange rind.

Pour batter into prepared pan. Bake for 25 to 30 minutes or until a wooden pick inserted in center comes out clean. Cool in pan on wire rack 10 minutes, then remove from pan, and cool completely on wire rack.

While cake is cooling, make frosting. Beat cream cheese, butter, powdered sugar, and vanilla together until smooth and fluffy. Add a teaspoon or two of milk if frosting seems too stiff. Refrigerate until needed. When cake is completely cool, spread on frosting with a butter knife, swirling appropriately. Press chopped pecans around the sides.

Pisces

Feb 19 - Mar 20

Symbol: Double Fish

Element: Water

Ruler: Neptune

Quality: Mutable

Riding the Waves

Dreamy Pisces, swimming through life. Imaginative, idealistic, sympathetic: these floating romantics don't mind wallowing in sentimentality, even to the point of putting on rose-colored glasses for viewing the one they love.

Remember, though, that their feelings are close to the surface—although they thrive on romance, emotional storms are easily triggered even by small slights. Pisces are classic water signs, flexible, intuitive, empathetic, and drawn to the sea. Their colors are sea-greens, blues, and silvers; water lilies, willows, irises, and ferns are their plants. Their sign, the double fish (occasionally drawn as two fish connected at the mouth by a cord), comes from the Babylonian zodiac, symbolizing the goddesses associated with the two great life-giving rivers of Babylon; the Tigris and the Euphrates. Ruled by the distant planet Neptune, named for the Roman ruler of the seas, Pisces dive deep and roll with the waves.

Like Gemini, the other dual sign, Pisces can often seem to have two distinct sides to their personalities, or to be under the sway of abruptly shifting moods. Like the weather over the ocean, they can go from sunny and calm to dark and brooding without much outward cause. They're not capricious; they just have a strong emotional current running through their veins, which makes them lightening rods for whatever storm clouds might be gathering on the horizon. As a result, Pisces often does best with a solid, grounded partner who can roll with their mood shifts.

Intellectually vibrant, observant and creative, these fish can swim in both directions at once as visionaries, poets, artists, philosophers, and scientists of all stripes. (Copernicus, Schopenhauer, Alexander Graham Bell, Jean Renoir, Rudolph Steiner, Albert Einstein, Jack Kerouac: Pisces all.) Faced with a problem, they'll happily spend days on end in the lab or studio exploring the possibilities, and their intuitive nature often leads them to inventive solutions never imagined by their more earthbound colleagues. They often express themselves creatively in the arts as well, although they're most productive when they have some rules, or at least a steady hand on the tiller, to guide them and keep their tendency to drift in check.

Like water, they are mirrors, reflecting back the attitudes and desires of their surroundings, their partners and their friends. Watch out, though: although they may seem endlessly pliable and accommodating, they're keeping track of just how much attention and romance you're delivering. Come up short, and space-case Pisces might surprise you with just how fast she can pack up and hit the road. A perfect soul-mate is what compassionate, sensitive Pisces longs for and believes in.

No matter how many times a romantic ideal might disappoint them, they'll keep on their quest, believing the truth—and their one and only—is still out there, just waiting to be found. They're no lightweights in the loving department; they're more likely to get swept to the altar than settle for a casual hookup. (Elizabeth Taylor: she of the 8 husbands, glittering rocks and outsize emotions? A Pisces.)

How to win the hearts of these water-loving wanderers? Curious as they may be, their mermaid's palate recoils from anything too spicy, funky, or weird. Pamper and please them with cool, delectable dishes with a tang of the sea and a hint of sunshine. Go for romance: Pisces loves to be treated right, and where other signs might be embarrassed by the full monty of roses, candlelight, and Barry White, Pisces will see it as a sign of dedication and true caring. They'd do it for you, so step up and do it for them. Polish up the nice china and good glasses, for sure, but don't limit yourself to the dining room. Lay out a glamorous picnic on the rooftop, or set up a table under the stars outside. Keep their mind entertained, and their heart (and body) will follow.

Menu

Crab Cakes
Slow-Roasted Arctic Char
Herb Salad
Fingerling Potato Salad
Lemon Fluff

Crab Cakes

Always a tasty and festive little treat, spritzed with lemon and eaten fresh from the pan.
To keep the coating crisp, fry these up right before serving.

1/3 lb fresh crabmeat, drained and picked over to remove any bits of shell
1/3 cup mayonnaise
2 tsp grated lemon rind
1 tsp lemon juice
1 tbsp minced fresh chives
2 generous pinches of salt and freshly ground black pepper
1/4 cup panko (Japanese bread crumbs), plus 1 cup for dredging
2 tbsp butter or vegetable oil, for frying
lemon wedges

Using a rubber spatula, lightly mix crab, mayonnaise, lemon rind and juice, chives, salt, and pepper together.
Stir in 1/4 cup panko crumbs.

Shape into 4 small patties. Spread remaining cup of panko on a plate. Dredge patties in crumbs, turning over to coat evenly. If you have time, cover patties with plastic wrap and chill for one hour in the fridge. Melt butter in a large non-stick pan. Add patties and cook over medium-low heat for 4 to 5 minutes on each side, until golden brown on the outside and hot within. Blot on paper towels and serve with lemon wedges.

Note: Panko (Japanese bread crumbs) are very light, dry, and crunchy, making them perfect for dredging these moist little cakes. Look for them in the Asian section of a well-stocked supermarket. Can't find them?
Very fine cracker crumbs (like pulverized Saltines) can be substituted.

Slow-Roasted Arctic Char

Coral-colored arctic char is milder and less rich than salmon, with a texture reminiscent of rainbow trout.
Using slow, damp heat keeps it moist and supple.

1 lb Arctic Char filet, skin on (or salmon, if unavailable)
2 shallots, peeled and minced
2 tbsp minced dill
2 tbsp minced flat-leaf parsley
grated rind of 1 lemon
salt and pepper to taste
1/4 cup olive oil

Preheat oven to 275°F. Mix shallots, herbs, lemon rind, olive, salt and pepper into a paste. Plaster fish with this paste on both sides. Lay in a long glass baking pan and put in the oven on the center rack. Put an additional pan half-filled with hot water on the lower rack. Let cook very slowly for 20 to 25 minutes, until fish is moist but cooked through, and will flake when poked with a fork. Peel off the skin and chunk the fish over a mound of Herb Salad. Surround with Fingerling Potato Salad.

Herb Salad

A fresh, aromatic mix of feathery bits of dill, chervil, and parsley, tossed with asparagus tips, small waxy potatoes, arugula or watercress, and sliced garden radishes. Adjust the herbs to taste and availability; mint, basil, and cilantro would also work well here.

a small handful of fresh dill, thick stems removed
a small handful of fresh flat-leaf parsley, stems removed
a small handful of chervil
1 branch fresh tarragon, leaves stripped from stalk (optional)
1/2 bunch asparagus, bottom third removed
1 bunch arugula or watercress, thick stems removed
1 bunch radishes, tops and tails removed, sliced
2 tsp white wine or champagne vinegar
2 tbsp extra-virgin olive oil
salt and freshly ground pepper

Toss herbs together. Drop asparagus into a saucepan of boiling water, and cook until bright green and just beginning to bend, about 2 to 3 minutes. Drain in a colander and run cold water over asparagus to stop the cooking. When asparagus are cool, pat dry and slice thinly, leaving tips whole. Toss asparagus, arugula, and radishes with herbs.

Just before serving, toss with olive oil, salt and pepper until leaves are lightly coated and shiny.
Sprinkle on vinegar and toss again. Taste for seasoning.

Fingerling Potato Salad

If you can't find fingerling potatoes (the name given to a family of curved, thumb-sized, rather waxy potatoes), use the smallest red-skinned boiling potatoes available.

1/2 lb fingerling potatoes, such as La Ratte, Banana, Austrian Crescent, or Rose Finn Apple

2 tbsp minced chives

2 tsp white wine vinegar

1 tsp Dijon-style mustard

2 tbsp olive oil

salt to taste

Cover potatoes with cold salted water and bring to a simmer. Simmer until just fork-tender. Drain in a colander. While potatoes are cooling, whisk vinegar, mustard, oil, and salt together. When potatoes have cooled off enough to handle, slice in half lengthwise and toss with chives. Drizzle on dressing and toss to coat.
Grind on some fresh black pepper just before serving.

Lemon Fluff

It's light! It's fluffy! It's sunshine in a cup! Piled up in glass parfaits or wine glasses, this make-ahead dessert is happy yellow, sweet with just a hint of tart. If you live on the West Coast (lucky you!) and can get your hands on some Meyer lemons, use them by all means—you'll get an extra-sweet and fragrant fluff. But any kind of lemons would be fine, too. Bottled lemon juice will not do—I don't care if it's organic and came from the health food store, that bitter nasty stuff will not work here. (Of those cute but vile plastic squeezy lemons, the less said, the better. And don't even think about faking it with lemon Jell-O.) Put your shoes on, go to the store and buy some fresh lemons. Roll them between your palms to soften them up and make them easier to juice. Mmm, don't your hands smell good? Look for Knox unflavored gelatin next to all the little flavored Jell-O boxes. Trust me, it's there, if only for the wacky people who dissolve it in water and drink it to harden their nails.

2 tsp unflavored gelatin (such as Knox)
3 tbsp cold water
4 eggs, separated
juice of 2 lemons
2/3 cup plus 3 tbsp sugar
1/8 tsp salt
Topping (optional): 1 fresh mango and 1 kiwi, peeled and diced

Sprinkle gelatin over water and set aside to soften. In double boiler over simmering water, beat egg yolks & lemon juice with a whisk or hand-held electric mixer until light and fluffy. Gradually add the 2/3 cup sugar and the gelatin, beating until slightly thickened. Remove from heat and let cool. Beat the egg whites until foamy, then add salt. Keep beating until soft peaks form. Add 3 tbsp sugar gradually and beat until stiff but not dry. Fold egg whites into custard, folding gently but thoroughly until mixture is uniform. Spoon into serving dishes and chill for several hours or overnight. Top with diced kiwi and mango just before serving.

Acknowledgments

For all the real-life, lifelong friends and family whose endearing traits were shamelessly plundered for astrological inspiration. Mountain-climbing Aries rams Amy, Jen, Rob, Julie P. and Susie B. Karlyn and Kristen, the best Taureans I know. Christina, Emma, Lanette, and Shifra, unforgettable Geminis all. Jackie and Jane, rock star Cancers, and Bea, Bella, Graham, Pam and Sally, fabulous Leos. Brunch-loving Virgos Katie, Melisa & Chris, Mom, and Molly. David, Mike, Paige, Shar, and Susie K., my favorite Libra party people. Noir-loving Scorpios Jet and Roxxie. Karalee, Scott, and Dad, smart and trusty Capricorns. And, of course, Michele the Pisces, and Aquarians Leslie J. and Eric S. And of course, many thanks to Jen Joseph, for tea, sympathy, lunch at Lunch, and believing that Manic D really did need a cookbook on the list.

Ingredient *Index*

Shrimp Scampi, 58
Spicy Tofu, 37
Stuffed Winter Squash, 90

Side Dishes

Farro Pilaf with Dried Mushrooms, 102
Pepperonata with Zucchini, 59
Pickled Peaches, 111
Red Cabbage, 91
Salsa, 45
Sautéed Bok Choy, 39
Southern Cheese Grits, 110
Sweet Potato Hash, 68
Tomato sauce, 57
Yam Balls, 47

Yogurt dip, 74

Desserts & Baked Goods

Baklava, 75
Cake
Black Tart, 104
Bleeding Heart, 84
Hummingbird, 112
Winter Pear Galette, 93

Cookies

Lemon Bars, 33
Madeleines, 53

Custard, 48
Fudge sauce, 40
Ice cream sundaes, 40
Lemon fluff, 120
Muffins, 66
Tiramisu, 61

Cooking Measurement
Equivalents

Liquid Measures

1 cup = 8 fl. oz. = 1/2 pint = 237 ml.

2 cups = 16 fl. oz. = 1 pint = 474 ml.

4 cups = 32 fl. oz. = 1 quart = 946 ml.

2 pints = 32 fl. oz. = 1 quart = 0.964 liters

4 quarts = 128 fl. oz. = 1 gallon = 3.784 liters

dash, less than 1/4 teaspoon

Dry Measures

3 teaspoons = 1 tablespoon = 1/2 ounce = 14.3 grams

2 tablespoons = 1/8 cup = 1 oz. = 28.3 grams

4 tablespoons = 1/4 cup = 2 oz. = 56.7 grams

5 tablespoons + 1 teaspoon = 1/3 cup = 2.6 oz. = 75.6 grams

8 tablespoons = 1/2 cup = 4 oz. = 113.4 grams (1 stick butter)

12 tablespoons = 3/4 cup = 6 oz. = .375 pound = 170 grams

32 tablespoons = 2 cups = 16 oz. = 1 lb. = 453.6 grams

64 tablespoons = 4 cups = 32 oz. = 2 lbs. = 907 grams

Notes